Writers in the Secret Garden

Learning in Large-Scale Environments

Justin Reich and Nichole Pinkard, editors

Writers in the Secret Garden: Fanfiction, Youth, and New Forms of Mentoring, Cecilia Aragon and Katie Davis, 2019

Writers in the Secret Garden

Fanfiction, Youth, and New Forms of Mentoring

Cecilia Aragon and Katie Davis

The MIT Press
Cambridge, Massachusetts
London, England

This book was set in ITC Stone Serif Std and ITC Stone Sans Std by Toppan Best-set Premedia Limited. Printed and bound in the United States of America.

Library of Congress Cataloging-in-Publication Data is available.

ISBN: 978-0-262-53780-3

10 9 8 7 6 5 4 3 2 1

For Dave, Diana, and Ken

For our students, who make coming to work every day a joy

For all the fanfiction authors, who inspire us with their creativity and willingness to share

Contents

Series Foreword

Learning across the life span is more important than ever, and with the wealth of resources and communities available online, there has never been a better time to be a learner. Learners of all ages—in formal and informal settings—are turning to online tools to help them develop new skills and knowledge for work, school, and leisure. The field of large-scale learning engages in the study of networked environments with many, many learners and few experts to guide them.

Large-scale learning environments are incredibly diverse: massive open online courses (MOOCs), intelligent tutoring systems, open learning courseware, learning games, citizen science communities, collaborative programming communities, community tutorial systems, social learning networks, and countless informal communities of learners on platforms such as Reddit, YouTube, and fanfiction sites. These systems either depend upon the direct participation of large numbers of learners in a single instance, or they are enriched by continuous improvement based on analyzing data generated by many learners over time. They share a common purpose—to increase human potential—and a common infrastructure of data and computation to enable learning at scale.

Technologies for large-scale learning are sometimes built deliberately, as in the case of MOOC platforms, and they are sometimes adapted from technologies originally developed for other purposes, as in the case of video-sharing sites. In some cases, they are used by individual learners around the world, and in other cases, large-scale learning environments are embedded within more traditional and small-scale educational systems such as classrooms and schools. They can be used to foster human capacity and create new opportunities, but they can also be used to teach and spread hateful ideologies. With a capacious enough definition of learning, large-scale learning technologies are implicated in nearly every part of the human experience in the networked world, from schooling to professional learning to politics to health care and beyond.

The Learning in Large-Scale Environments series from the MIT Press seeks to investigate, critique, and explain these large-scale environments and the various ways they are hybridized with residential learning space. Just as large-scale learning environments are diverse, our series includes books with a diverse set of methodological and theoretical perspectives, ranging from learning science to computer science to sociocultural research traditions. The series examines large-scale learning environments at multiple levels, including technological underpinnings, policy consequences, social contexts and relationships, learning frameworks, and the experiences of educators and learners who use them. Our hope is that researchers will find valuable contributions to the scholarly literature and that educators and policy makers will find useful insights as they consider how best to support the learning needs of students of all ages around the world.

Justin Reich
Nichole Pinkard
Series Editors, Learning in Large-Scale Environments

Foreword

Casey Fiesler

It's easy to focus on all the terrible things that networked technologies have brought into our lives—misinformation, harassment, polarization, automated inequality. These are all things that pull us farther apart rather than bring us together, but it doesn't have to be that way. This book describes one such counternarrative, an example of how the same affordances of the internet that allow for those negative experiences have also created and nurtured a *positive* community that has touched countless lives—including mine.

When I first logged on to AOL as a teenager in the mid-nineties, one of the first things I remember searching for in this exciting new online world was *Star Trek*. From AOL I stumbled onto Usenet, and then alt.startrek.creative, and that's where I discovered *fanfiction*. It felt like something clicked into place for me; through sharing my own *Star Trek* stories, I found a writing community and, in fact, a learning community. I didn't have the words to describe it then, but the positive feedback that helped me grow as a writer was an example of the distributed mentoring described in this book.

As the internet became an increasingly important part of our lives, it also became an important topic for scholarly research that teaches us not only about technology but also about our world and ourselves. From communication to education to computer science and beyond, a variety of academic fields have explored how online platforms such as Wikipedia, Stack Overflow, and Scratch serve as communities where people can share, learn, and connect. As I moved through research communities myself, I was surprised not to see more people paying attention to fanfiction writers and readers as another remarkable example of an online community—one that might even have lessons for how to make our other networked spaces more welcoming and positive.

So when I first saw Cecilia Aragon presenting some of her and Katie Davis's first work on this topic, a detailed ethnography subtitled "Thousands of Positive Reviews," I wanted to jump up and down for joy. They had captured precisely what I thought everyone needed to know about fanfiction communities—the positivity, the learning experiences, the social benefits, and more. The type of mentorship they describe was something I experienced myself, improving my own writing with the help of constructive feedback and, even more importantly, encouragement. I have a number of friends who are now successful published authors and who got their start in fanfiction—and more still who are writing fanfiction read by tens of thousands of people.

The concept of distributed mentoring described in this book captures what makes online fanfiction communities such ideal spaces for informal learning. The sheer abundance of feedback, the variety of perspectives, the cumulative nature of learning, the persistent availability of experiences to learn from, and the positive norms surrounding critique have all evolved from the combination of the culture of fanfiction and the affordances of networked technologies. Taken together, those "thousands of positive reviews" have contributed to the education and support of countless young people who have improved their writing and made important social connections while doing so.

In addition, the social norms that Cecilia and Katie describe in the context of distributed mentoring influence not just feedback around writing but the entire culture of the community. In my own work, I have done extensive research around the fanfiction platform Archive of Our Own (AO3), which is itself a wonderful example of what fanfiction communities can create. AO3's founders built their own platform from scratch in 2008, and today it has almost 2 million users. They also designed it with the values of their community—respect, positivity, and inclusiveness—in mind. Just as Cecilia and Katie's research participants describe fanfiction as a "labor of love," the same is true of the archive itself. Even developers I interviewed—all women, a stark contrast to other open source projects—described the learning environment (this time for coding, not writing) as "loving." Similar to the stories of young people who found that supportive encouragement from the fanfiction community spurred them to improve their writing, the same kind of social relationships helped more women learn to code.

As you will learn in this book, fanfiction communities also include a large number of young people who are creating and learning and even teaching. They are proof that young people can accomplish amazing things—not just through their creativity but also through collective action. For example, the fan activist group the Harry Potter Alliance has mobilized tens of thousands to advocate for causes such as human rights and literacy. Fanfiction writers also advocate for themselves; the nonprofit Organization for Transformative Works (which also supports AO3) has helped shape copyright policy to support fair use.

These communities are also inclusive spaces where young people can be themselves and geek out about the things they love in a place where they'll be celebrated for it. Fanfiction communities can even function as important support spaces for LGBTQ teens who may not have this support elsewhere in their lives. The story in the introduction of this book of an isolated teen who found a vital social outlet in fanfiction communities is just one of countless more. Over the course of my research, I've heard multiple stories about how these communities literally save lives.

Fanfiction, fan communities, and "geek" culture are becoming more mainstream, and fan studies—an interdisciplinary field that crosses media studies, literature, cultural studies, gender studies, and social science—is also beginning to touch fields such as computer science. This book builds upon a long history in fan studies of drawing attention to the depth, appeal, and power of both fanworks and the communities that create and surround them; however, the concept of distributed mentoring is something new. By combining ethnography and data science, Cecilia and Katie have been able to rigorously establish and detail something that will ring true to anyone familiar with fanfiction as well as provide new insights that will help fans see their communities in a new light while also illustrating how much the rest of the world can learn from them.

This book is a wonderful example of such a cross-disciplinary learning opportunity. Fanfiction communities might showcase the power of distributed mentoring, but as readers will discover, this concept could have much broader applications. Creativity bubbles up from every corner of our networked spaces—from artwork (DeviantArt) to knitting (Ravelry) to modding games (*Minecraft*). When you combine these creative projects with a community of people who share a similar passion and knowledge, the result is a community of learning as well. This book provides deep insights into

one organically successful example—and thus a roadmap for how designers might better support distributed mentoring in other online affinity
spaces.

As someone who spent some time as a teenager in the "secret garden" of
fanfiction communities myself, I can attest to their transformative power.
I hope that many more young people get to have that same experience.
Maybe they'll find it in the new kinds of affinity spaces—ones that bring us
together rather than pull us apart—that this book can help inspire.

Acknowledgments

The ideas we've generated in this book have been shaped by years of discussion with dozens of people whose names may not all be mentioned here. We are grateful in particular to the members of the fandom communities who have shared their stories with the world and, in so doing, enriched ours.

Our editor at the MIT Press, Susan Buckley, deserves credit for being the one who first approached us with the idea of writing a book on this topic. She went on to provide invaluable support throughout the writing process.

This book would never have been written if not for the hard work and excitement of our talented students at the University of Washington:

- The students in our first fanfiction directed research group in 2013—Sarah Evans, Julie Ann Campbell, Abigail Evans, and David Randall—spent nine months and hundreds of hours conducting a detailed ethnography into three fandoms.

- We are especially grateful to Sarah Evans, now an assistant professor at Texas Woman's University, whose enthusiasm and contributions to the project have extended over five years.

- John Frens came up with the original idea of comparing lexical diversity with abundance of reviews, implemented much of the software, and conducted rigorous statistical analyses to find the correlations.

- Ruby Davis, fanfiction author and student researcher extraordinaire, generously allowed us to share her personal story throughout this book.

- Kodlee Yin wrote tools to collect much of the fanfiction data and incorporated differential privacy into our database to protect the young creators.

- Jihyun Lee, Deepa Agrawal, Niharika Sharma, Diana Zhang, and Meg Drouhard contributed software, data analysis, and visualizations.

We are grateful to Heather Jean Uhl, our initial librarian informant in 2013, who gave us inspiration and confirmation that our research interests were worth pursuing.

We thank all our interview and survey participants for enthusiastically sharing their experiences with us.

At the University of Washington, we wish to thank the Information School (UW iSchool) and the Department of Human Centered Design and Engineering for providing significant support and a home for our research. We are also grateful for the existence of the DUB (Design, Use, Build) community, which provided the initial conditions (lunch) for our first meeting. In addition, we had fruitful conversations with UW colleagues, including Brock Craft and many others.

The UW iSchool GA Crew provided us with superb editing and formatting assistance under tight deadlines. Specifically, we are appreciative of Julianne Peeling's attention to detail in completely formatting all references and editing the final manuscript of the book. Marie Williams Chant, Jesse Van Hoy, and Julia Hon did a fantastic job wrangling our first-draft references on short notice.

At the MIT Press, our editor's assistant, Noah Springer, and production editor, Liz Agresta, provided ongoing support throughout the editorial process. We also thank the anonymous expert reviewers from the MIT Press for their helpful ideas, which greatly strengthened the book.

Most of all, of course, we wish to thank our families, in particular Cecilia's daughter, Diana, who first introduced her to fanfiction and provided many insightful ideas, and her son, Ken, who convinced her that writing and vocabulary could be learned from online games as well as printed books. Katie wishes to extend a special thanks to her stepfather, Gordon Johnson, for flying to Seattle specifically to look after her son, Oliver, so that she could make our deadline to MIT.

1 Introduction: The Secret Garden

The internet has opened up unprecedented opportunities for people of all ages to discover and connect with others who share their interests. Among the most popular interest-based communities are those that bring together fans of various media texts, including movies, TV shows, music bands, novels, and video games. Whether formed around classics (such as *Star Trek*, *Doctor Who*, or *Blade Runner*) or newer media texts (such as *Breaking Bad*, the *Twilight* series, or *World of Warcraft*), these online fan communities make it easier than ever before for people to meet other fans and engage in discussions and creative endeavors around their mutual interests.

In the past twenty years, amateur fanfiction writers, often young people between the ages of thirteen and twenty-five, have published an astonishing amount of fiction in online repositories. Measured by words alone, this quantity rivals the 80-billion-word Google Books English-language fiction corpus covering the past five centuries. A single online repository alone, Fanfiction.net, included nearly 7 million stories comprising 61.5 billion words, more than 176 million reviews, and over 1.5 million authors in February 2017 (Frens, Davis, Lee, Zhang, & Aragon, 2018). Far from mere shallow repositories of pop culture, these sites are accumulating significant evidence that sophisticated informal learning is taking place online in novel and unexpected ways (Black, 2006, 2007, 2008; Campbell et al., 2016; De Kosnik, 2016; Evans et al., 2017; Fiesler, 2008; Hellekson & Busse, 2014; Jenkins, 1992, 2006).

In this book, we explore how young people are utilizing new forms of technology to mentor one another in writing fanfiction and developing their writing skills. For the past five years, we, along with over a dozen students in our research group, have been conducting mixed-methods research of online fanfiction repositories and combining our respective skills in data science and education to develop a novel melding of techniques that demonstrate the effectiveness of the new field of human-centered data science. We conducted a nine-month ethnographic study of two fanfiction sites, including in-depth interviews of fanfiction authors, the observation of online fanfiction discussion groups, the analysis of reader reviews, and even writing our own fanfiction. In the process, we discovered a new kind of mentoring, which we call *distributed mentoring*, that is uniquely suited to networked communities, where people of all ages and experience levels engage with and support one another through a complex, interwoven tapestry of cumulatively sophisticated advice and informal instruction. We continued to iterate our research, performing large data analysis through a human-centered lens, collecting quantitative data to deepen and enhance our qualitative understanding of the phenomenon of distributed mentoring. We focused not only on the observation of distributed mentoring in fanfiction communities but also on the process of human-centered data science that we used to comprehend it. We further considered the evidence for the existence of distributed mentoring beyond fandom, for example, in sites focused on art (such as DeviantArt) or knitting (such as Ravelry) and perhaps other venues where informal or formal education takes place.

This book will be of interest to educators in schools, after-school programs, libraries, and other community settings who want to apply the principles of distributed mentoring to collaborative learning experiences that improve writing skills and foster critical thinking; to scholars and students in education, digital media, digital humanities, human-centered data science, and related fields; and to anyone with an interest in fanfiction or online youth communities.

In this introduction, we discuss why we chose our methods to study online fanfiction and why we believe this study is important, including the chance encounter that initiated our research project and the personal experiences that made it particularly meaningful to us. We then introduce the concept of distributed mentoring and conclude with a brief outline of the book.

Genesis of the Book

The ideas in this book were sparked when we (Cecilia Aragon and Katie Davis) met for the first time at a University of Washington event in Seattle in March 2013 and struck up a casual conversation over lunch. Cecilia is a computer scientist with research interests in data science and online collaboration, and Katie is a specialist in digital youth, child development, and education. That year, it seemed many pundits were claiming that young people had become incapable of long-form writing and only used technology for shallow interactions. Both of us felt something was wrong with this conclusion, because we each had close teenage relatives whose writing abilities defied these stereotypes. In particular, the young people we knew described heavy involvement in fan communities and fanfiction reading and writing. This apparent contradiction struck us as fertile ground for potential research, and thus began a multiyear ongoing collaboration that would lead us in surprising directions.

Our research project would eventually span over five years of mixed-methods research, including in-depth ethnographic studies and computational analyses of vast data sets. It would grow to involve a dozen students and several faculty members and would uncover a new kind of mentoring uniquely suited to networked communities, which we named distributed mentoring. But as we delved deeper into fanfiction communities and the millions of young people who actively participate in reading, writing, identity development, and community building, we discovered that not only was a great deal of informal learning and mentoring taking place but also powerful and unexpected developments were occurring in fanfiction communities that had the potential to improve young people's lives far beyond merely helping them to develop literacy and communication skills.

A Personal Note: A Tale of Two Teenagers

One of the undergraduate students in our research group, Ruby Davis (no relation to Katie Davis), told us, "When I started writing fanfiction in 2010, at age thirteen, I was a queer, autistic middle schooler who had not yet realized that she was either of these things. I had difficulty with many of the social situations that came naturally to others my age, and I became isolated from my peers at school. Fanfiction communities were a vital social outlet for me. I struggled with verbal communication at that age, so written digital communication was a way for me to finally feel like I could express myself and communicate in an effective and creative way."

Today, Ruby is a confident and skilled writer and a graduating senior at the University of Washington. When I (Cecilia) first met her and welcomed her into our research group, I was struck by her poise and confidence. I couldn't help contrasting her experiences in adolescence with my own struggles in middle school as a shy, first-generation Latina daughter of immigrants growing up in small-town Indiana. At times bullied and ostracized, I regularly went days without speaking to a single person in school, and I was so physically and socially awkward that I had to sneak peeks at my classmates to see what they were doing with their arms and hands in social situations. More than anything else, I remember feelings of isolation and loneliness and a profound conviction that something was wrong with me. Why else did my classmates ridicule me and my teachers relegate me to the slow reading group? Why did my middle school math teacher tell me to stop working so hard in class and instead try to get a boyfriend? I had no close friends in middle school, and for many years there was no one to whom I could communicate my most deeply held feelings and beliefs. I had no words to form my own identity and no mentors, no connections with anyone like me. And yet I loved to write and would often express myself in long, rambling stories that I never showed anyone. These included what I now realize was fanfiction, stories that transformed the genders or motivations of characters from my favorite books. When I think of the healing and joy that I could have found in an online fanfiction community, had one existed at that time, it's almost unbearable. The contrast between the possibilities today and the isolation I experienced growing up is stark. It took me several decades to overcome the corrosive effects of racism, sexism, and loneliness to achieve my own sense of identity and self-confidence.

But today, Ruby and millions of others like her in online fanfiction communities around the world are finding their own identities, learning about life, building community, and developing critical skills that are necessary for thriving in the interconnected twenty-first-century world. Ruby writes, "Today, I see fanfiction—and fandom in general—as fundamental to my culture, identity, and community. All of my closest friends both in the physical and virtual worlds are fannish, and fandom has shaped my gender identity, sexual orientation, and political ideologies. Fanfiction is a way I can give back to this community of people, and it's important to me to continue feeding the fannish ecosystem. I create fanfiction today to have fun, feel productive, receive validation, express my ideas, practice my writing skills, explore characters I love, and bring joy to others."

Hearing a young person describe her experience in fanfiction communities with such passion and joy gives us tremendous hope. Alongside all the well-documented negative effects of the internet on adolescents, including the consequences of their highly interconnected and occasionally far too public lives, we hope to provide a contrasting view. However, we need to emphasize that our research is limited in its application to fandom even if we do attempt to identify broader implications beyond it. We studied only two fanfiction sites (Fanfiction.net and FIMfiction.net) out of many, and we make no claims that our discoveries of a highly supportive community are representative of fandom in general. In particular, although our findings are quite positive, it has been documented that abuse and harassment have occurred on many fanfiction sites (Dym & Fiesler, 2018; Guerrero-Pico, Establés, & Ventura, 2018). Nevertheless, although we don't wish to diminish the risks or gloss over the negative effects, it can't be denied that opportunities for community and connection exist that never have before, especially for young people from marginalized backgrounds. Furthermore, we believe our findings may be extended more broadly to wherever network-enabled mentoring takes place in a supportive community, which we will explore in the final chapter.

So our work has become more to us than a research project into an understudied but important online phenomenon. It's become deeply personal and incredibly exciting. We hope our discoveries may bring additional insight into how young people learn; help change some of the popular views of digital youth and the much-maligned sphere of fanfiction production; and perhaps even inspire designers to construct online affordances that enable isolated young people to establish connections, facilitate greater learning and discovery, and find community.

A New Approach to Data Science

One of the challenges for scholars attempting to investigate online fanfiction is the extraordinarily vast scope of the text: tens of millions of novel-length stories on a single repository alone, with more being produced each day on many multifandom and single-fandom repositories alike. Assuming a normal human reading rate of 250 words per minute sustained over four hours per day, it would take a reader well over three thousand years simply to peruse the existing stories, much less to study and reflect upon them— not to mention the fact that new chapters and stories are being added to the collection at a prodigious rate. Clearly, it's impossible for a person even to skim all this fiction, let alone read and ponder the hundreds of millions of reviews discussing the stories.

When faced with this apparently insurmountable volume of text, one research approach may be to treat such masses of text solely as data and utilize computational approaches to allow researchers access to broad assemblages of text corpora. This may be considered a data science approach to understanding human-generated text. Similarly, scholars in the digital humanities may apply computational techniques to study research questions over large text corpora, whereas others critique the use of digital tools as a replacement for individual scholarship (Dinsman, 2016; Svensson, 2010).

Literary scholar Franco Moretti has proposed the controversial method of "distant reading," a purely computational practice to analyze literary texts via network analysis, natural language processing, and other algorithmic means (Moretti, 2000, 2013). Although his ideas have been met with some skepticism, it can't be denied that computational techniques have revealed a great deal about online text communication, social media, and other forms of human-generated text. Nevertheless, some of the insights extracted lack the rich detail that close reading, ethnography, and other qualitative approaches have brought to the understanding of text communication, literature, and other sociotechnical phenomena (Aragon et al., 2016).

Thus, we're left with a conundrum. We're dealing with a phenomenon encompassing millions of young readers and writers. We believe that the subtleties of how young people are learning to write via fanfiction communities, and how they teach one another through what we term distributed mentoring, can't be fully understood through a purely algorithmic approach. So how do we preserve the richness associated with traditional qualitative methods while utilizing the power of large text data sets? How do we uncover social nuances or consider ethics and values in the vast number of texts we are studying?

We believe that the answer lies in a carefully constructed, mixed-methods approach that utilizes the strengths of both qualitative and quantitative research, a technique that merges human subtlety with computational speed and rigor. This approach has been termed *human-centered data science*: an interdisciplinary field of study that involves the thoughtful merging of contextually grounded qualitative and ethnographic analyses with rigorously designed and implemented software tools derived from human-centered approaches.

We've found that neither a qualitative nor a computational approach suffices in and of itself, yet a significant amount of care is required to merge the two approaches. It's not sufficient to sample blindly, diving into a sea of text to read at random, fettered by unconscious biases, nor is it enough to slap together a Python script to scoop up vast quantities of words without fully understanding the nuances, humor, politics, social webs, and fragile connections between the humans producing these stories. Nor should one mix these two approaches naively without careful study of the underlying phenomena. The best tactic appears to lie in an intelligent combination of the two techniques, as has been studied in fields such as human–computer interaction, visual analytics, interactive machine learning, and computational social science, where human input provides valuable feedback to computational results through an iterative and highly interwoven process whereby each discovery builds upon the results of the previous one and is in turn modified by these results, over and over again.

Nevertheless, this combination technique requires significant expertise and depth of knowledge in at least two mature fields of study. Thus, collaborative approaches to such research projects are most likely to achieve the best results, given that human time is limited and that each of us has at best only a few decades on this earth to hone and refine our skills. This is one reason why we feel that our collaboration has been so fruitful. Our story began, as do so many stories of discovery, with the creativity sparked by human connection.

As mentioned earlier, we (Katie and Cecilia) had come from very different backgrounds when we met for the first time at an event organized by the University of Washington DUB (Design, Use, Build) community, "a grassroots alliance of faculty, students, researchers, and industry partners interested in Human Computer Interaction & Design" (DUB, n.d.). Katie had focused her research on digital youth, whereas Cecilia had studied informal text communication in online communities. Katie, a professor in the Information School at UW with a doctorate in human development and education from Harvard, possessed a rich background in mixed-methods studies of young people online. Cecilia, a professor in the Department of Human Centered Design and Engineering with a PhD in computer science from UC Berkeley, originally came from the data science and computational tradition but had also studied online collaboration among both children and adults. It seemed at the time that we were surrounded by conventional wisdom decrying the supposed fact that young people were incapable of long-form writing (Bradshaw, 2004; Gardner & Davis, 2013; Turkle, 2011). However, we both had young family members whose writing abilities defied these stereotypes. We began our research collaboration to investigate this apparent contradiction.

In September 2013, we formed a directed research group at the University of Washington and were joined by graduate students Julie Ann Campbell, Sarah Evans, Abigail Evans, and David Randall. Together, we conducted an in-depth, nine-month ethnographic investigation of online fanfiction communities, including participant observation and fanfiction author interviews. Our study led to the discovery of a new type of mentoring facilitated by networked publics that we termed distributed mentoring (Campbell et al., 2016). Further research continued in the years to follow, with data science master's students Deepa Agrawal, Niharika Sharma, and Diana Zhang; human-centered design and engineering PhD students Meg Drouhard, John Frens, and Jihyun Lee; and undergraduates Kodlee Yin and Ruby Davis contributing to a constellation of research projects over a period of five years (for more details of our research, see Human-Centered Data Science Lab, n.d.). During this time, Sarah graduated with a PhD in education from the University of Washington and joined the faculty at Texas Woman's University, while continuing to contribute to this project. Colleague Brock Craft, a senior lecturer in human-centered design and engineering at the University of Washington, joined our group to contribute ideas in visualization and visual analytics. Under our direction, Kodlee, an informatics undergraduate, led a software-engineering project to collect a complete snapshot of Fanfiction.net authors, stories, reviews, and metadata. Niharika, Deepa, and Diana performed visual analytics and data science on this vast array of text and networked data. John contributed the novel idea of examining lexical diversity over time among fanfiction authors and found a correlation with reviews received. Ruby, John, and

Diana investigated the network structure of fanfiction authors and reviewers by performing social-network analysis and looking into comparisons with Dunbar's number in face-to-face communication.

In this book, we describe the results of the research we've conducted together with these students and colleagues. This body of work illustrates the power of the techniques of human-centered data science as applied to fanfiction texts. Understanding the progression of our work over time may be helpful to others who wish to take a human-centered data science approach to studying large qualitative data sets.

Book Outline

We begin the remainder of this book with a brief history of both fanfiction and mentoring in chapter 2 to provide context for our work. With its roots dating to popular television shows of the 1960s such as *Star Trek*, fanfiction has blossomed into an extremely widespread form of creative expression. The transition from printed zines to online fanfiction repositories facilitated this explosion in popularity, with millions of fans authoring stories and contributing to sites such as Archive of Our Own (AO3), Fanfiction .net (FF.net), Wattpad, AdultFanfiction.net, LiveJournal, DeviantArt, Tumblr, FIMfiction.net, Fiction Alley, and many others. Enthusiasts are sharing their writing, reading stories written by others, and helping one another to grow as writers. Yet this domain is often undervalued by society and understudied by researchers. Mentoring, on the other hand, has been studied exhaustively by researchers and educators, but there is still disagreement on exactly what constitutes a mentoring relationship. We consider this research and provide new evidence for the rise of a novel form of online mentoring, distributed mentoring.

In chapter 3, we turn in detail to our theory of distributed mentoring, exactly how it occurs, its seven attributes (abundance, aggregation, accretion, acceleration, availability, asynchronicity, and affect), and how each of these attributes is being utilized by young people to engage one another in writing and learning. Each of these characteristics is supported by networked technologies. *Abundance*, for example, describes the sheer volume of feedback accessible to the author. *Availability* evokes the reviews' persistent and public nature, which facilitates sustained exchanges and relationships among community members.

Chapter 4 describes our in-depth ethnography in detail. In 2013, our initial approach to studying and understanding the fanfiction community was ethnographic as we sought to learn what writers, primarily adolescents and young adults, were gaining from their participation in fanfiction communities. We observed multiple instances of individuals stating their overall writing skills had improved due to their involvement in fanfiction and remarking upon the value of mentoring in their achievements.

As we began our research, we expected to find traditional mentoring relationships with experienced authors teaching younger or less experienced writers. Instead, we discovered a phenomenon that went beyond the standard definitions of mentoring. We found that fanfiction authors (often young people) are publishing stories that may be several hundred thousand words in length, sometimes exceeding the length of the original works on which they are based. Readers are offering encouragement and constructive feedback on stories, which authors use to improve their writing. All of this happens in a predominantly supportive community atmosphere that stands in stark contrast to the negativity and even hate speech found on so many online sites (e.g., Reddit, 4chan, comments posted on news sites) (Moore, Nakano, Enomoto, & Suda, 2012). Authors experience mentorship from the community, grow as writers, gain recognition for their work, and form meaningful connections with other fans.

Chapter 5 presents further evidence for distributed mentoring via the first quantitative analysis of its type of the 61.5 billion words of fiction on a single fanfiction repository, Fanfiction.net. This data set includes 672.8 GB of data, consisting of 6,828,943 stories, 8,492,507 users, and 176,715,206 reviews. To quantitatively test the theory of distributed mentoring using this massive corpus, we longitudinally tracked lexical diversity over stories as authors received feedback, utilizing the Measure of Textual Lexical Diversity (MTLD) as our primary metric. MTLD captures the use of unique words in a text, and previous research has demonstrated that this measure correlates with human judgments of writing quality (Crossley, Salsbury, McNamara, & Jarvis, 2011; Mazgutova & Kormos, 2015). We examined lexical diversity in English-language stories produced by 301,226 writers, primarily young people, and found that MTLD scores increased as the authors received reviews, even when we controlled for the effects of popularity, aging, and practice (Frens et al., 2018). These results supported the theory of distributed mentoring and produced implications for designers of informal learning communities. Through this unique mixture of data science, interactive visualization, and qualitative analysis, we found evidence of improved skills that were influenced by community participation.

Throughout chapter 5, we describe in detail the process of our human-centered data science approach and how we came to meld qualitative and quantitative techniques to obtain a more complete picture of a highly networked ecosystem of online fanfiction, a community that research group member Ruby Davis calls "a mutually supportive environment that encouraged us to continue creating alongside one another." This iterative approach enabled us to form a deeper understanding of distributed mentoring as it occurs in Fanfiction.net. We hope this chapter in particular will be helpful to scholars wishing to study similarly large networked communities or other massive collections of human-generated data.

Finally, in our conclusion in chapter 6, we extend our gaze beyond fandom to explain how distributed mentoring may be used to improve the writing experiences of youth outside fanfiction communities. We list three fundamental insights we've gleaned from our research and describe the practical implications for design with a focus on educators and developers of online learning platforms. We suggest ways that parents and educators can contribute to a positive mentoring experience and help engage young people in developing their writing skills. We explore potential applications of distributed mentoring to online communities outside of fanfiction and identify three key ingredients that must be present. And last, we speculate on the implications of our theory for formal education and present suggestions for the transformation of writing instruction in schools today.

It's our hope that the research and ideas we express in this book may spark further discussion in multiple communities and add to the growing body of evidence of the power of informal learning in interest-fueled communities. Above all else, we hope that our work may help ensure that fewer marginalized young people experience an adolescence like Cecilia's and that more of them find connection, community, and identity like Ruby.

2 The History of Fanfiction and Mentoring

What Is Fanfiction?

Fanfiction is a type of transformative creation in which fans of a variety of different media—including television shows, movies, comic books, anime, and video games—produce stories based on the original media while expanding upon or altering them. Fanfiction authors may construct plot trajectories deviating from the original text, explore untold background stories, or place the characters in an alternate universe altogether different from the canonical setting. Fanfiction stories may vary in length from one-shots of less than one thousand words to novel-length tales or even multimillion-word epics.

The first recorded use of the term *fanfiction* dates to the early science fiction fandom of the 1930s (Speer, 1944). But if we take a wider definition of the act of building upon other authors' stories, filling in the gaps of existing narratives, creating complexity, and speculating more deeply about relationships between fictional characters, we can argue that the phenomenon has been going on since the first humans told stories to one another in purely oral traditions. Building upon others' work is a fundamental human characteristic and a tradition in creative, scientific, and religious institutions throughout written history.

John Lydgate's *The Siege of Thebes*, written in 1421, was a sequel to Chaucer's *Canterbury Tales*, which in turn was based on earlier stories, such as Boccaccio's *Decameron*. From the late 1800s through the early 1900s, authors wrote derivative works based on Lewis Carroll's stories. Fans of Jane Austen and Sir Arthur Conan Doyle wrote and distributed their own stories in the early 1900s, and they continue to do so today (Jamison, 2013;

Romano, 2010; West, 2014). It's well known that Shakespeare often borrowed his plots and characters. Milton's *Paradise Lost* is derived from narratives and characters in the Bible. Talmudic scholars added commentary to their sacred texts (Barenblat, 2014; West, 2014).

It's a common experience that adult readers and fans of today, when remembering their childhood, recall instances of building on or transforming books, movies, television, or other media texts, particularly to incorporate alternative viewpoints or give voice to marginalized populations. When Cecilia first read J. R. R. Tolkien's *The Lord of the Rings* as a child of ten, she was so frustrated by the lack of female main characters that she reimagined the entire story by regendering several of the characters. This is not an uncommon development, as has been documented by numerous fans, including one quoted in a popular online fan wiki, Fanlore: "As far as I figure it, 'fanfic' has been something that has probably existed in every kid's life. ... I can recall stories I made up about [*Star Wars,*] ... and my friend and I used to make up stories about [*Star Trek*] as we rode down the bike path every afternoon. ... The only difference now is, more people share their work with others" (quoted in Fanfiction, n.d.).

Lawrence Lessig (2008) has argued in *Remix* that this type of "Read/Write" or remix culture is as old as human history and that it is only in the twentieth century that we have created laws to prevent this type of remixing, thus moving from a "Read/Write" to a "Read-Only" culture. In that sense, Lessig suggests, we learn about creativity by learning how to write. We take, use, build upon others' works without permission and have done so for centuries (Lessig, 2004, 2008).

Nevertheless, fan scholars (Bacon-Smith, 1992; Coppa, 2006; De Kosnik, 2016; Hellekson & Busse, 2014; Jenkins, 1992) agree that despite variants in the definition of the term, fanfiction underwent a significant change in the 1960s. The modern incarnation of what has been called fanfiction or transformative work has its roots in this decade, when the widespread introduction of television and other forms of mass media brought shared cultural texts to unprecedented numbers of people, notably including the widespread popularity of the television series *Star Trek* and the growth of its fandom (Bacon-Smith, 1992; Jenkins, 1992; Reich, 2015).

As Joshua Meyrowitz has argued, "Electronic media have changed the significance of space, time, and physical barriers as communication variables" (1985, p. 13). No longer are people's immediate experiences of story limited to face-to-face, individualized encounters (Goffman, 1959). As this has occurred, the innate human tendency to build structures upon works of the imagination that captivate us emotionally has been reinforced and enhanced by the ability to connect with others who share the same cultural experiences. Fanfiction has become a shared cultural activity, a community creative effort (Hellekson & Busse, 2006).

Kristina Busse, founding coeditor of the journal *Transformative Works and Cultures*, contends that community is key to what makes fanfiction interesting (Bell, 2015; Busse, 2015). She prefers as a scholar to focus on the modern incarnation of fanfiction, its collaborative and community nature. Busse and Karen Hellekson argue in *The Fan Fiction Studies Reader* that there are many ways to define fanfiction. If defined as

> a form of collective storytelling, then the *Iliad* and the *Odyssey* might be tagged as the earliest versions of fan fiction. ... If the term requires an actual community of fans who share an interest, then ... fan-written [Sherlock] Holmes pastiches [would serve] as the beginnings of fan fiction. Finally, if we look at it as a ... rewriting of shared media, in particular TV texts, then media fan fiction, starting in the 1960s with its base in science fiction fandom and its consequent zine culture, would start fan fiction proper." (Hellekson & Busse, 2014, p. 6)

Regardless of the definition of the term, fanfiction today is worthy of study if only for the sheer numbers of people, particularly young people, who participate as readers and creators of this new type of remixed content. The prodigious quantity of creative content on a single fanfiction repository alone, produced over the past twenty years on Fanfiction.net, approaches the amount contained in the Google Books fiction corpus, which strives to collect all fiction ever published since the beginning of recorded history.

The amount of fanfiction produced continues to grow explosively. Fanfiction.net authors were producing 80,000 new narratives per month in 2013, while at the same time, the total number of fiction books published or self-published by authors in the United States stood at 3,600 books per month (De Kosnik et al., 2015; De Kosnik, 2016, p. 336). In other words, on a single archive alone, fanfiction writers were producing more than twenty-two times the number of fiction books issued by US publishers. And even that extraordinary rate of story production on Fanfiction.net has recently become significantly dwarfed by that of AO3, currently the fastest-growing fanfiction archive in the world (De Kosnik, 2016).

To put this staggering amount of creative production in context, De Kosnik writes,

> At a rate of one story per day, it would take ... 14,907 years to read all of the stories, in all 8,000+ fandoms, on FF.net. ... The number of reviews posted to stories on FF.net (139.5 million) over the past fifteen years is greater than the number of people who bought tickets to sporting events in the United States and Canada, inclusive of all games played in the National Football League, National Basketball Association, Major League Baseball, and National Hockey League, in 2012 (131 million). ... This is a rate that no other traditional media industry or entertainment genre can match. (De Kosnik, 2016, p. 342)

By January 2017, Fanfiction.net had grown to contain over 6.8 million stories by nearly 1.5 million unique authors, 8.5 million members, and over 177 million story reviews (Yin, Aragon, Evans, & Davis, 2017). AO3 currently contains over 2 million fanfiction works and has accrued over 750,000 users (Fiesler, Morrison, & Bruckman, 2016). But it is not simply its popularity that makes fanfiction worthy of investigation; it is what people are doing on fanfiction sites—and how they are benefiting—that merits empirical inquiry.

We believe that the experiences and activities of young people today, who are producing and consuming creative content by others, have far-reaching implications for youth literacy and connected learning (Gee, 2013; Ito et al., 2010; Lankshear & Knobel, 2007). Young people are publishing novel-length stories. Readers are offering encouragement and constructive feedback on stories, which authors use to improve their writing (Black, 2007; Campbell et al., 2016; Evans et al., 2017; Parrish, 2007). And surprisingly, we found that this occurs in a primarily positive online community where "flames," or nonconstructive negative reviews, constitute less than 1 percent of comments on a random sample of Fanfiction.net stories (Evans et al., 2017).

Previous work, as well as our research, has documented the benefits that people gain through their participation in online fanfiction communities. Authors experience mentorship from the community, grow as writers, gain recognition for their work, and form meaningful connections with other fans (Black, 2006, 2007, 2008; Campbell et al., 2016; Chandler-Olcott & Mahar, 2003; Coker, 2008; Evans et al., 2017; Fiesler, Morrison, & Bruckman, 2016; Hill, 2016; Hills, 2002; Hinck, 2012; Jenkins, 1992, 2006; Johnson, 2014; Lammers, 2014, 2016; Lammers & Marsh, 2015; Larbalestier,

2002; Mathew & Adams, 2009; Veale, 2013). Additionally, and perhaps even more importantly for young people engaged in the process of identity formation, fanfiction communities provide a space for marginalized members of society—particularly women, nonbinary genders, and people of color—to explore and develop identities at odds with mainstream cultural narratives (Altintaş, 2013; Baker-Whitelaw & Romano, 2014; Busse & Hellekson, 2006). Indeed, some of the literary explorations taking place in fanfiction in the sixties and seventies, such as romantic relationships other than heterosexual—at the time, often viewed as "deviant"—may now be more generally accepted by society (Baker-Whitelaw, 2014; Baker-Whitelaw, 2015; Busse, 2017; Jenkins, 2012). Thus, trends in fanfiction today may be harbingers of the future of literature or society.

Jenkins notes in *Textual Poachers* that "the emergence of media fandom can be seen, at least in part, as an effort to create a fan culture more open to women, within which female fans could make a contribution without encountering the entrenched power of long-time male fans; these fans bought freedom at the expense of proximity to writer and editors" (1992, p. 48). Further, "fan reception cannot and does not exist in isolation, but is always shaped through input from other fans and motivated, at least partially, by a desire for further interaction with a larger social and cultural community" (p. 76).

Nevertheless, fans and fanfiction have often been viewed negatively by society. As Jenkins comments, "fans operate from a position of cultural marginality and social weakness" (1992, p. 26). We believe that this negative perception is on the cusp of widespread change. One marker of this sea change has been the growing number of academic studies of this phenomenon. Informal conversations with undergraduates also appear to confirm this changing public view of fanfiction, particularly among young people, who often openly discuss their fic reading and writing behavior with friends face-to-face. Our student Ruby articulated a view we've heard echoed widely among young people:

> In my early days, I didn't want people to know that I read or wrote fanfiction or that I participated in fandom at all. I can remember one specific time in my first year of high school when a friend and I exchanged DeviantArt accounts, and I spent the next several days having an existential crisis about it. I considered changing my username or deleting my account. At some point in high school, though, I started trying to be more open about my online accounts in fandom

spaces. Sharing my Tumblr with real-life friends was stressful at first, but ultimately it was an important step towards becoming comfortable with myself and open about who I am. Today, I don't hide my affiliation with fandom. Although I still keep my online handle private, I have no hesitation about sharing that handle with my friends. In fact, many of the people I interact with in fandom spaces are friends of mine in the physical world.

Today, fanfiction studies is an expanding academic field that traces many of its origins to the early nineties, beginning with seminal work by Henry Jenkins, Camille Bacon-Smith, and others. Jenkins's influential study of television fans, *Textual Poachers*, examined fanfiction history and culture in several of its chapters (Jenkins, 1992). Bacon-Smith argued in her book *Enterprising Women* that women were finding community and developing writing and creative skills through sharing fanfiction (Bacon-Smith, 1992). Since then, the number of scholarly works on fanfiction has exploded, and many overviews of fanfiction and its culture have been published.

Fan scholars have examined fanfiction from numerous angles. Fiesler, Tushnet, Nolan, Stendell, and Stroude, among others, have explored legality and copyright issues concerning fanfiction (Chatelain, 2012; Fiesler & Bruckman, 2014; Fiesler, Feuston, & Bruckman, 2015; Fiesler, Lampe, & Bruckman, 2016; Halbert, 2006; Katyal, 2006; Latagne, 2011; McCardle, 2003; Musiani, 2011; Nolan, 2006; Schwabach, 2009, 2011; Stendell, 2005; Stroude, 2010; Tushnet, 1997, 2009, 2017). Feminism and identity among fanfiction authors and readers have been discussed in numerous works (Bury, 2005; Busse, 2015; Busse & Hellekson, 2012; Fiesler, Morrison, & Bruckman, 2016; Hellekson & Busse, 2014; Merrick, 2009). Chandler-Olcott and Mahar (2003) and Mathew and Adams (2009), among others, have examined the educational potential of fanfiction (Hurtado, Engberg, Ponjuan, & Landreman, 2002; Jwa, 2012; Mackey & McClay, 2008; Roozen, 2009). Many others have focused on sexuality and its exploration (Hampton, 2015; Jenkins, 1992; Johnston, 2015; Penley, 1997; Scodari, 2004; Tosenberger, 2008).

In 2014, Karen Hellekson and Kristina Busse published *The Fan Fiction Studies Reader*, a collection of articles by leading fan scholars discussing fanfiction as literary artifacts, issues of identity and feminism, affect in fanfiction, and the role of creativity and performance in fandom. Busse produced a collection of her own essays in 2017, *Framing Fan Fiction: Literary and Social Practices in Fan Fiction Communities*, which focuses on identity, feminism, and community within fandom.

Abigail De Kosnik (2016) has considered fanfiction repositories as "rogue archives" and has stated that an ever-growing portion of our cultural memory, the discussion of popular media, is being archived not by central authorities but by amateurs uploading content. She has studied fanfiction repositories from a media studies perspective and has examined the concept of the archive in the age of the internet.

Rebecca Black (2006, 2007, 2008) has studied language acquisition and identity formation among English-language learners writing fanfiction. Black has analyzed connections between authors and readers in the form of story reviews. She has found that such interactions help authors shape their learning space and identity.

Young academics are entering the field after an adolescence spent reading or writing fanfiction. For example, Brittany Kelley's 2016 PhD dissertation focuses on online fanfiction communities and takes a feminist approach to addressing identity, emotion, ethics, and literacy in these spaces. She remarks on the inspiration for writing in general and for her academic work that she found through her encounters with fanfiction: "I found a writing community—the first real writing community I had ever encountered— that left me feeling refreshed, excited, and invigorated. It made me want to write" (Kelley, 2016a, p. 3).

Online fanfiction communities have proliferated and grown rapidly since the early 1990s. Single-fandom and multifandom repositories have appeared, grown, and fallen into disuse accordingly, as interest in the source texts waxes and wanes. Today, the primary multifandom archives include Archive of Our Own (first launched in 2008 and since 2013 the fastest-growing fanfiction repository), Fanfiction.net (the current largest fanfiction archive, begun in 1997), Wattpad, DeviantArt, Tumblr, AdultFanfiction.net, and others. Examples of single-fandom repositories, or sites exclusive to fanfiction written for one particular fandom, include FIMfiction.net (*My Little Pony*), A Teaspoon and an Open Mind (*Doctor Who*), Fiction Alley (*Harry Potter*), STARS Library and Twilighted (*Twilight*), and many, many more, too numerous to name here. It's likely that any even moderately popular media source, whether television, movies, anime, books, comics, games, or another format, has spawned a fanfiction site maintained by dedicated amateurs. Nevertheless, the current trend appears to be toward centralized, multifandom repositories.

De Kosnik notes that fans "transition[ed] from a phase of highly centralized archives (from the mid-1990s to the early 2000s) to a phase of decen-
tralized archiving in the early rush of social media (during the 2000s), and
around 2007, the concept of a central archive—which AO3 explicitly calls
itself—became dominant in fandom once again" (2016, p. 93). The advantage of a central archive is easy to see: As the quantity of fanfiction becomes
ever vaster, it becomes more and more difficult to find the type of fiction
fans might prefer to read, especially if they transition from one fandom to
another over time. Central repositories, particularly AO3, with its sophisticated system of tagging, facilitate this process. Based on previous research
(Campbell et al., 2016; De Kosnik, 2016; Hellekson & Busse, 2014; Kelley,
2016a), it appears that readers in their teens may find Fanfiction.net first
and begin reading, posting, learning, and mentoring there. As they become
more sophisticated in their fandom and fanfiction knowledge, they transition to AO3 primarily because of its design and stated goals as "a fan-
created, fan-run, non-profit, non-commercial archive for transformative
fanworks" (Archive of Our Own, n.d.).

AO3 was launched in 2008 by female programmers and fans who felt the
need for control over their own creations. Fiesler, Morrison, and Bruckman
present an excellent overview of the impetus to create AO3:

> In 2007, in the wake of YouTube's massive success and among the wave of
> start-ups dedicated to user-generated content, a group of men created a website
> intended to monetize content that a community of mostly women had been
> sharing amongst themselves for free. FanLib, a for-profit archive for fan fiction …
> was heavily criticized by the existing community of writers, who viewed it as at
> best tone-deaf to their values and at worst a deliberate attempt to exploit. (2016,
> p. 2574)

Fiesler, Morrison, and Bruckman believe that AO3's dramatic growth is
largely due to its successful application of both user-centered and value-
sensitive design.

The user demographics of Fanfiction.net and AO3 are very different.
Although 90 percent of the members of both archives self-identify as female
or nonbinary gender, we found the median self-reported participant age on
Fanfiction.net is sixteen (Yin et al., 2017). This is confirmed by the internet
data site Alexa, which reports that visitors to Fanfiction.net are primarily
school age and female (Alexa, 2017). Qualitative research describes typical

users of AO3 as longer-term adult fans, with a median age in their thirties (De Kosnik, 2016).

Fanfiction.net has been characterized as having a "reputation for hosting fic primarily written by younger, 'feral' fans" (De Kosnik, 2016, p. 93). Thus, we chose to center our study on Fanfiction.net precisely because of its younger demographic. In this book, we are not attempting to duplicate the many excellent studies of online fandom or fanfiction history but rather to focus on both the burgeoning use of fanfiction among adolescents and young adults as a means of developing literacy and writing skills within a supportive community and also the value of this type of informal mentoring and support for young people's learning.

As we will explore in this book, we believe that encounters with fanfiction, contrary to popular negative beliefs, inspire and support young people today—particularly members of marginalized groups—to develop literacy, to support one another in positive ways, and to teach and learn through new types of informal learning and mentoring. As Kelley explains, "The investigation of online fanfiction spaces is especially valuable for rhetoric and composition because it highlights how writing is a deeply embodied and emotional, life-long (learning) process" (2016a, p. 11).

We focus on young people aged thirteen to twenty-five years, who may have recently discovered fanfiction and who are still developing their skills in literacy and learning to write, including adolescents in the process of identity formation. Our emphasis lies in the development of mentoring and writing skills, on what young people teach and learn in these communities.

Our research group's ethnographic study recognized that fanfiction communities are a form of what Gee describes as "affinity spaces," or "interest-driven passion-fueled site[s]" (2013, p. 174). We found that in fanfiction communities, "personal differences in age, gender, or class are less important than the shared interest being explored. ... [N]ovices become experts through guided participation in the social structure of the community" (Campbell et al., 2016, p. 692).

Many researchers have noted the unique types of learning exchanges taking place in fanfiction communities. Bacon-Smith explains that women writers encounter nurturing communities where they can practice their creative skills (1992), and Kelley finds that these communities also validate "more 'feminized' writing practices, such as collaboration, friendly support, and an unapologetic focus on romantic themes" (2016a, p. 18). Kelley goes on to note that "these writers are involved in some sort of affective exchange" (2016a, p. 2) and confirms our finding of the importance of affect in learning by explicitly agreeing with our conclusion that emotion and affect are "key to expanding our understanding of community literacy practices that take place outside of school" (p. 161). This process of learning is particularly important for marginalized writers, such as women, people of color, and members of the LGBTQIA+ community.

In this book, we focus on the engaged participation of youth in fanfiction production and on how young authors are mentoring one another via a type of community-based learning uniquely facilitated by the technological affordances of networked publics that we call distributed mentoring.

A History of Mentoring

As with fanfiction, Homer serves as an apt starting point for investigations of mentoring. In the *Odyssey*, when Odysseus leaves to fight in the Trojan War, he entrusts the care of his son, Telemachus, and his palace to his old friend, Mentor. The goddess Athena disguises herself as Mentor when she visits Telemachus and in that guise gives him advice about going in search of his father. Today, we use the term *mentor* to refer broadly to someone who imparts wisdom and guidance to someone less experienced.

People have supported one another's learning and growth throughout human history, but scholarly writing about mentoring dates back only to the 1970s (Irby & Boswell, 2016). This work emanates primarily from the fields of education, business, and psychology (Crisp & Cruz, 2009). Studies in these fields typically explore formal relationships established between a more experienced (often older) mentor and a less experienced (often younger) mentee, with the express goal of supporting the specific educational, professional, or personal goals of the latter (Blackwell, 1989; Bozeman & Feeney, 2007; Brown, Davis, & McClendon, 2000; Haggard, Dougherty, Turban, & Wilbanks, 2011; Jacobi, 1991; Levinson, 1979; Murray, 2001; Roberts, 2000). Here, we consider a wider range of and contexts for mentoring relationships.

Compared to fanfiction, mentoring has received greater attention from scholars and educators since it became a focus of study in the 1970s. And yet, there is still considerable disagreement about what exactly constitutes a mentoring relationship (Crisp & Cruz, 2009; Dawson, 2014; Hall, 2003). In their theoretical review of the education, business, and psychological literature, Crisp and Cruz identified over fifty definitions of *mentoring*. These definitions vary according to the scholar's discipline (e.g., business versus education) as well as how the word is used. For instance, some scholars use *mentoring* to refer to the activities conducted by a mentor, whereas others discuss mentoring as a process that is not necessarily tied to a designated individual.

The variety of definitions may relate to the familiarity of the word. We use *mentor* in everyday language to refer to various types of people who provide us with some kind of support. However, if pressed to operationalize our intuitive understanding, we might each put forward a slightly different definition. Our shared intuition gives rise to an imprecise definition. This challenge plagues researchers who study similarly familiar concepts, such as identity, learning, and motivation.

Despite the myriad definitions they identified, Crisp and Cruz (2009) nevertheless found areas of agreement among scholars. First, mentoring relationships provide support for a person's growth and accomplishment. Second, the type of support provided may take many forms, such as professional development, psychological support, and role modeling. Many scholars agree on two broad categories of support: instrumental and psychosocial (see Eby, Rhodes & Allen, 2010). Instrumental support refers to the coaching, information, and sponsorship involved in helping someone achieve specific professional or academic goals, whereas psychosocial support refers to the friendship, caring, and acceptance that helps impart self-esteem and self-efficacy to the person being mentored. There is less agreement on the specific activities that ought to be included in providing these different forms of support. Third, scholars largely agree that mentoring relationships are both personal and reciprocal, although some scholars emphasize that reciprocity does not translate to equality (e.g., Bozeman & Feeney, 2007; Keller, 2005).

Eby, Rhodes, and Allen (2010) compared mentoring relationships to other types of relationships, such as those with coaches, parents, friends, and counselors. Their comparison helps tease out distinct qualities of mentors that, when combined, produce a distinct form of supportive relationship. At the same time, the comparison highlights great diversity in the form, scope, and context of mentoring relationships. Mentoring relationships can arise in an academic, workplace, or community context; they can be initiated either formally or informally; their scope of influence can be academic, social, professional, or personal; the power differential between mentor and mentee can be large or small; and their emotional closeness can range from high to low. Moreover, there exists a wide range of people who can serve as mentors, including parents, community members, teachers, and peers (Higgins & Kram, 2001).

Rather than attempt to reconcile the disparate definitions of mentoring into a single, unifying definition, Dawson (2014) instead embraced the definitional variations and created a framework that accounts for many different forms and contexts of mentoring relationships. The framework presents sixteen dimensions along which mentoring relationships can be organized and conceptualized: objectives, roles, cardinality, tie strength, relative seniority, time, selection, matching, activities, resources and tools, role of technology, training, rewards, policy, monitoring, and termination.

In our prior work, our research team used Dawson's framework to classify the type of mentoring relationships we observed in our ethnographic research on fanfiction sites (Campbell et al., 2016). We observed that fanfiction sites feature mentoring that is informal, weakly tied, peer-based, many-to-one or many-to-many, and computer-mediated. Mentoring is often provided in a spontaneous, one-off way, making it informal and weakly tied. (Of course, this doesn't prevent engagement between particular authors from developing into a longer relationship; it just means this is not the default state of affairs.) Mentoring is peer-based because there is no formal hierarchy in fanfiction communities. Finally, the large number of participants on fanfiction sites makes possible a many-to-one or many-to-many experience that exists on a larger scale than simply having multiple mentors. Because of its multidimensional nature, Dawson's framework allowed us to label the supportive relationships we were seeing on fanfiction sites as mentoring relationships. Granted, the kind of mentoring we documented on these sites looks quite different from Mentor's relationship to Telemachus, but it was nevertheless distinct from coaching or friendship.

Of Dawson's sixteen dimensions, the *role of technology* was particularly salient to our work, but we found it somewhat underdeveloped theoretically. Drawing on Ensher, Heun, and Blanchard's (2003) typology of roles of computer-mediated communication (CMC), Dawson's primary distinction is in the degree to which CMC is employed in the mentoring relationship.

The possibilities range from non-CMC and CMC-supplemental mentoring models (where face-to-face relationships are dominant) to CMC-primary and CMC-only (where online relationships are dominant).

In their work, Ensher et al. identified five potential advantages associated with CMC mentoring versus face-to-face mentoring: "(1) greater access, (2) reduced costs, (3) equalization of status, (4) decreased emphasis on demographics, and (5) a record of interactions" (2003, p. 280). We draw on and expand this work by describing the distinct affordances associated with "fundamentally social technologies" (Stahl, Koschmann, & Suthers, 2006, p. 415) and the specific ways they support social interactions and group learning. These affordances include asynchronous communication, anonymity, and persistent, searchable content, among others. In the next chapter, we present our attempt to provide greater theoretical depth and clarity around the transformative role of networked technologies through our theory of distributed mentoring.

The Contexts and Outcomes of Mentoring

Much of the scholarly writing about mentoring focuses on formal mentoring programs that pair a more experienced person with someone less experienced (Eby et al., 2010). In business, scholars investigate the effectiveness of mentoring programs in workplace settings to determine whether such programs support the professional growth of workers and the overall success of the companies that employ them (Humberd & Rouse, 2016; Hunt & Michael, 1983). Workplace mentors typically provide two types of support: career-related support that helps mentees advance along the corporate ladder and emotional support that increases mentees' confidence in their professional abilities (Kram, 1985).

In higher education, studies explore mentoring programs that pair faculty members with undergraduate students, as well as programs that pair more senior students with incoming students. These studies focus on common markers of student success in undergraduate education, such as retention, grades, and adjustment to and satisfaction with college (Crisp & Cruz, 2009). Mentoring is also important in graduate education, where faculty members introduce graduate students to the norms and expectations of a professional field (Austin, 2002).

Youth mentoring is an area of scholarship that focuses specifically on children and adolescents. In youth mentoring relationships, an adult typically provides regular guidance and support to a young person in an effort to develop the youth's competence and character (Eby et al., 2010). This support can be instrumental, emotional, or both. Youth mentoring has an important role to play in the positive youth development (PYD) perspective, which focuses on youths' strengths rather than their deficits (Scales & Leffert, 1999; Silbereisen & Lerner, 2007). In fact, mentoring relationships have been identified as the single most important developmental asset that a community can provide its young people (Theokas & Lerner, 2006). Specific benefits associated with youth mentoring include improved academic performance and reduced risk behaviors (DuBois & Silverthorn, 2005; Erickson, McDonald, & Elder, 2009; Rhodes, Grossman, & Roffman, 2002; Rhodes & Lowe, 2009).

Youth mentoring relationships can be established through formal programs or in an informal, spontaneous way. Thousands of youth development programs exist in the United States alone that involve a mentoring component; some familiar examples include Big Brothers Big Sisters, Boys & Girls Clubs, Boy Scouts, Girl Scouts, and 4-H (Silbereisen & Lerner, 2007). These programs offer youth the opportunity to experience positive adult-youth relationships in the context of life-skill-building activities and participation in and leadership of valued community activities (Silbereisen & Lerner, 2007).

Whether in the workplace, school, or community, many mentoring relationships develop spontaneously, outside the many formal programs that exist in these contexts. And yet, there is relatively little research on informal mentoring, despite the fact that many youth claim to have informal mentors (Beam, Chen, & Greenberger, 2002). The research that does exist suggests that informal mentors can play a positive and influential role in young people's lives, offering both instrumental and emotional support (Barron, Martin, Takeuchi, & Fithian, 2009; Beam et al., 2002). For instance, Ko and Davis (2017) found that having a mentoring relationship was a stronger predictor of interest in computing than either gender or socioeconomic status among a diverse group of teens. In a subsequent study investigating a three-week career-exploration class, teens from underrepresented groups were invited to write extensively about their informal computing mentors (Ko, Hwa, Davis, & Yip, 2018). An analysis of their writing identified a variety of positive influences associated with informal mentors, including shifts in identity development and self-efficacy, interests and career goals, and perspectives about the world.

Insights from Research on Informal Learning

Research on young people's informal learning experiences provides valuable insight into the nature and impact of informal mentoring relationships. Two concepts from the learning sciences are particularly relevant to the fanfiction context: *communities of practice* (Lave & Wenger, 1991) and *affinity spaces* (Gee, 2004). In a community of practice, novices learn alongside experts in an apprenticeship model of informal learning (Lave & Wenger, 1991). When they are new to the community, novices engage in a process of legitimate peripheral participation where they observe more centrally positioned, expert members of the community. Through these observations, they learn about the community's social structure and practices, eventually moving themselves from peripheral to central members of the community.

Affinity spaces also involve novices and experts, but they place less emphasis on the idea of a community and its related questions of who belongs and does not belong to the group (Gee, 2004). Affinity spaces bring together people who share common interests or goals, rather than a common race, gender, or class. Affinity spaces recognize that each person brings a mix of skills to a particular shared experience. As a result, a person may act as an expert in one context and a novice in the other. In this way, the distinction between novices and experts is not as pronounced or meaningful as it is for a community of practice, where novices are moving toward a clearly defined conception of full participation (Black, 2008).

We find the perspective of everyone learning from everyone else particularly fitting for the fanfiction context and our theory of distributed mentoring. Fanfiction authors can be both apprentices and masters at the same time. They might have expertise in grammar or canon knowledge, which they share with others, but lack skill in character or plot development, for which they seek out others' guidance. Thus, we proceed with the understanding that fanfiction sites function as affinity spaces. In the following chapter, we consider how the affordances of networked technologies shape mentoring relationships in affinity spaces in unique ways.

Two additional concepts from the literature on informal learning are relevant to considerations of informal mentoring relationships: *participatory culture* (Jenkins, 2006, 2009) and *connected learning* (Ito et al., 2013). Jenkins defines participatory culture as "a culture with relatively low barriers to artistic expression and civic engagement, strong support for creating and sharing creations, and some type of informal mentorship whereby experienced participants pass along knowledge to novices" (2006, p. xi). The fanfiction sites that we investigated in our research have decidedly low barriers to entry—anyone of any age can choose to write and publish a story, just as anyone can review a story that has been published. The millions of story reviews provided by fanfiction readers suggest a high level of informal mentorship in fanfiction communities. We also discovered additional avenues for offering feedback in these communities, such as one-to-one, private messaging and writing forums focused on specific aspects of the writing craft (e.g., character and plot development) (Campbell et al., 2016). In all of these ways, fanfiction sites represent an excellent example of participatory culture. Our theory of distributed mentoring—discussed in the next chapter—deepens the current understanding of participatory culture in a networked era by describing the specific processes by which more experienced participants take advantage of networked technologies to offer informal mentorship to novices.

Distributed mentoring also draws on the connected learning framework proposed by Ito et al. (2013). This framework puts forward a view of learning that centers on personal interests and relationships and connects youth to opportunities for academic, civic, or economic achievement. The framework is useful for understanding how the development of authors' writing skills is fueled by their interest-driven, peer-supported experiences in fanfiction communities. Participants are drawn to fanfiction sites by a shared and deep interest in one or more fandoms and in fanfiction writing. Once there, they support one another's growth as writers. The theory of distributed mentoring shows how networked technologies shape the distinct forms that this peer support takes.

Conclusion

The explosive growth of online fanfiction has opened up a multitude of opportunities for new types of networked mentoring. When we first started studying these communities, we were struck by the astonishing varieties of creativity and peer support that had emerged among and between fanfiction authors. It was surprising to us at first that so much mentoring was going on within these particular types of affinity spaces. But as we deepened our ethnographic research and spoke with more young authors, we began to understand why these spaces were such fruitful sites for informal learning and mentoring.

As our student Ruby noted of her early experience, "We continually supported and encouraged each other to write and participate. We planned and executed story arcs for our characters, collaborated to decide which romantic relationships our characters would pursue, and shared research. ... Fanfiction became even more meaningful and important to me. It became a way for me to improve my writing skills, have fun, learn more about the world, and find community with like-minded people. My writing style changed, the way I engaged with media changed, and my world perspective changed." Ruby also observed that when she wrote every day and received daily supportive feedback, her writing "improved exponentially."

Her story is not unique, as we have discovered through our qualitative and quantitative research. In the next few chapters, we'll go into detail about how distributed mentoring works, present an in-depth ethnographic analysis of several fanfiction communities, and discuss how millions of young people today are benefiting from distributed mentoring online.

3   The Theory of Distributed Mentoring

Introduction

We developed our mentoring theory during an in-depth, nine-month ethnographic investigation of online fanfiction communities, including participant observation and fanfiction author interviews, along with students Julie Ann Campbell, Sarah Evans, Abigail Evans, and David Randall. Our study led to the discovery of a new type of mentoring facilitated by networked publics that we termed distributed mentoring (Campbell et al., 2016).

In our initial ethnography (described in more detail in chapter 4), we sought to learn what writers, primarily adolescents and young adults, were gaining from their participation in fanfiction communities. We observed multiple instances of individuals stating that their overall writing skills had improved due to their involvement in fanfiction and remarking upon the value of mentoring in their achievements. Based upon these observations, as we began our study, we expected to find experienced writers mentoring younger authors in primarily traditional mentoring relationships. Instead, we uncovered a complex, reciprocal network of advice that extended far beyond the conventional definitions of mentoring. We called this overall experience distributed mentoring. (Although others have applied the term *distributed* to mentoring to refer to mentors who are geographically distributed or remote [Computing Research Association, 1995; Khasnabis, Reischl, Stull, & Boerst, 2013; Sandherr, Roberson, Martin, Acholonu, & Nacu, 2014], we are invoking a different definition of the term here.) In this chapter, we describe the theory in detail, including its roots and a detailed description of each of its seven attributes: abundance, aggregation, accretion, acceleration, availability, asynchronicity, and affect.

Distributed Cognition

Our model is grounded in Hutchins's theory of distributed cognition, which takes as its base the assumption that knowledge may be distributed across individuals and artifacts and that the sum total of this knowledge is both greater than and qualitatively different from the knowledge inherent in any one person or object (Hollan, Hutchins, & Kirsh, 2000; Hutchins, 1995; Hutchins & Klausen, 1996). Based on Hutchins's background in anthropology and his extensive observations of ship navigation and crew coordination, he came to realize that "groups must have cognitive properties that are not predictable from a knowledge of the properties of the individuals in the group. ... [H]uman cognition is always situated in a complex sociocultural world and cannot be unaffected by it" (1995, p. xiii).

Hutchins makes it clear that cognitive activity must be located in context, where "context is not a fixed set of surrounding additions but a wider dynamical process of which the cognition of an individual is only a part" (1995, p. xiv). Further, the knowledge required to carry out a cognitive task may not be contained within individual minds but shared among team members. Thus, the humans in the system "act as a malleable and adaptable coordinating tissue, the job of which is to see to it that the proper coordinating activities are carried out. ... This amounts to a restructuring of functional systems that transcends the individual team members" (p. 219).

In distributed mentoring, mentoring processes are dispersed within the system of humans and artifacts in the environment, just as occurs with cognitive processes in distributed cognition. Mentoring systems emerge as a complex structure is formed that extends beyond any single individual or mentoring pair. However, distributed mentoring expands the concept of distributed cognition due to its focus on mentoring processes as influenced by networked technologies' distinct affordances.

We found that distributed mentoring stretches Dawson's (2014) framework of traditional mentoring models in unexpected ways within the informal structure of online fanfiction communities. For example, framework elements such as selection and matching of mentoring relationships, which are crucial components of most traditional models, were completely self-driven within the communities we studied. In our prior work, we explained that mentoring roles, number of relations, ties, and seniority varied both by individual and by task. For example, one person could offer mentoring in proofreading while receiving mentoring in plotting. On Fanfiction.net, there was no mentorship training, rewards were primarily intrinsic, and all monitoring was crowdsourced. Yet it was clear that thousands of authors were receiving and offering highly effective mentorship within these fanfiction sites on a daily basis. "Therefore," we concluded, "a new mentoring model is happening that is uniquely supported by the affordances of networked technologies and for which we must account" (Campbell et al., 2016, p. 699).

The benefits associated with distributed mentoring are very similar to those derived from distributed cognition. Distributed mentoring produces artifacts that are embodied outside the author, such as forum responses, reviews, private messages, and author's notes. These artifacts, as in distributed cognition, allow for the coordination of mentoring efforts. In addition, the wide access to information allows for error checking that may take the form of concurrence, disagreement, or discussion among respondents, exactly as in a cognitive system. The result is that the whole of the distributed mentoring experience ends up being greater than the sum of its parts. Multiple mentors and distributed artifacts create a richer mentoring experience than a single mentor alone could offer, similar to the cognitive processes observed by Hutchins where distributed cognition allows the accomplishment of tasks that could not be achieved by any one individual.

Participants in online fanfiction communities can be of any age and any experience level and often do not take on specific roles of master or apprentice, because their skill sets may be uneven. One author might possess considerable expertise in, say, canon knowledge but lack the ability to use English grammar correctly. Another might be skilled at characterization but have difficulty with plot construction. This diversity of experience and skill level is of benefit to the participants in distributed mentoring as each individual brings a unique perspective to their feedback, and the combination of human advice and material artifacts in the network provides a more nuanced and complete level of mentoring.

In particular, we found that reciprocity played an important role in the communities of fanfiction authors we studied. Because distributed mentoring is peer-based rather than hierarchical, an author receiving assistance on one topic can turn around and give critique to another author in a different area. Writers whom we interviewed noted that the help they had received inspired them to help others (Campbell et al., 2016). Over and over again, we found authors demonstrating this reciprocity. As our student Ruby observed, "It was a mutually supportive environment that encouraged us to continue creating alongside one another. ... I started out leaving mostly short, shallow, positive comments but gradually began writing more and more detailed comments to mimic the reviews I liked to receive on my own fanfic."

The nature of such mutually supportive networks lends itself to the development of more complex support structures. In addition, we found that authors are aware to some extent of the "connective tissue" that exists in their collaborative space. Similar to Hutchins's ship navigators and other participants in affinity spaces, the fanfiction writers in our study frequently made reference to the shared context of their participatory culture. A substantial proportion of the reviews we analyzed in Campbell et al. included elements of fandom discussion, which provided evidence that authors and reviewers shared a common foundation of knowledge: "Indeed, their shared knowledge goes beyond what is represented in the canonical literature to include fan canon notions of untold character backstories, favored relationship pairings, and popular plot conspiracies. Our analysis suggests that the communitarian ethos present in the civil, reciprocal exchanges in online fanfiction communities is likely encouraged by the membership that authors feel as participants in the community" (2016, p. 700).

Networked Technologies and Distributed Mentoring

Distributed mentoring is made possible by the distinct qualities of networked technologies. Much of networked communication is *text-based* and *asynchronous*, allowing people to communicate across geographic and temporal boundaries. Provided one has access to an internet connection and the necessary hardware, it's a trivial matter to connect with people many thousands of miles and time zones away. Due to the quality of asynchrony, conversations may stretch out over many days, weeks, months, and even years, lending an *always-on* feeling to computer-mediated communication (Turkle, 2011). In the process, a *persistent*, *searchable*, and *replicable* record of these text-based online exchanges is created (Aragon, Poon, Monroy-Hernández, & Aragon, 2009; Aragon & Williams, 2011; boyd, 2007a; boyd, 2007b). Persistence makes it possible to return to an exchange of ideas as many times as one desires. It's also possible for others to search for and discover the exchange then copy and share it with people who were not originally part of it. In this way, any single act of online communication is *scalable*, meaning it can be deployed in multiple contexts, by multiple people, and for multiple purposes (Walther, 1996, 2011).

Due to these characteristics of networked technologies, online communication has a decidedly public quality to it. A stark example of this public quality can be seen in Katie's study of girls' blogging on LiveJournal (Davis, 2010). The girls who participated in the study, most of them in late adolescence and emerging adulthood, told Katie how they had used LiveJournal as an online diary to record their daily thoughts, feelings, and experiences during middle and high school and into college. Unlike a traditional paper diary, however, their online diaries were visible to other people, many of whom the girls did not know personally offline. In fact, they weren't entirely sure of the full range of people who were reading their LiveJournal posts. The public quality of their writing had an influence on how they wrote and what they chose to share; many of them observed that they modulated their expressions based on how they wanted to portray themselves to their real and imagined audiences. The awareness of an audience also served a motivating function, as the girls enjoyed the idea that other people cared about what they had to say and sometimes even responded to their writing by leaving comments (typically supportive and encouraging). In this way, LiveJournal transformed a traditionally private, individual act—keeping a diary—into a public, social one.

Being public does not preclude *anonymity*—or at least the feeling of anonymity. In the early days of the internet, actual anonymity was considerably easier to achieve than it is today. Fewer people were online, digital photos—including selfies—were more difficult to take and upload, and social network sites such as Facebook, LinkedIn, Twitter, and Instagram did not yet exist. There was not the expectation there is today that the people with whom one interacts offline almost surely have an online presence and can be found easily through a Google search. Two cartoons from the *New Yorker*, published over twenty years apart, highlight the difference between the internet of the early 1990s and the internet of today. In 1993, Peter Steiner published a cartoon showing two dogs, one sitting at a computer, the other looking up at him from the floor. The caption reads, "On the Internet, nobody knows you're a dog" (Steiner, 1993). In 2015, Kaamran Hafeez published an updated cartoon showing two dogs sitting on the floor, talking to each other as their owner sits in front of his computer. The caption reads, "Remember when, on the Internet, nobody knew who you were?" (Hafeez, 2015). This second cartoon underscores the difficulty of achieving anonymity on today's internet. Social media platforms such as Facebook and LinkedIn are predicated on connecting one's online and offline identities. Indeed, research on young people's online identity expressions reveals a trend over the years toward less experimentation and greater alignment with one's offline identity (Davis & Weinstein, 2017).

Despite this trend away from true anonymity, there still exist ample opportunities to feel anonymous online. In our research exploring young people's digital media use, many of the youth we interviewed commented on feeling less inhibited when communicating with others online due to the absence of the typical nonverbal cues associated with face-to-face communication (Gardner & Davis, 2013). They explained that not having to look at someone directly as they typed made them feel less "seen" and therefore freer to express themselves without the typical self-censorship they practiced offline. This sentiment was particularly true for youth who participated in less mainstream online communities, such as fanfiction communities (Davis, 2010). Anonymity is more easily achieved on these sites due to the fact that members often don't know one another offline, as they do on sites such as Facebook, and they typically present a pseudonymous identity consisting of an avatar instead of a profile picture and a pseudonym instead of their real name (Busse & Hellekson, 2012).

The qualities of networked technologies discussed here—asynchrony, persistence, anonymity, etc.—present distinct opportunities and challenges for participating in online communities. Jenkins (2009) has identified eleven skills—which he calls "new media literacies"—that one must develop in order to participate effectively and responsibly in participatory cultures: play, performance, simulation, appropriation, multitasking, distributed cognition, collective intelligence, judgment, transmedia navigation, networking, and negotiation. All of these skills are relevant to the practice of distributed mentoring in fanfiction communities, but a few are particularly useful to keep in mind as we delve into the specific attributes of distributed mentoring in the next section.

Distributed cognition and collective intelligence relate most obviously and directly to the practice of distributed mentoring. In the context of new media literacies, distributed cognition involves being able to recognize the

affordances of the tools and platforms associated with networked technologies and to use them to accomplish one's goals (Jenkins, 2009). *Collective
intelligence* takes advantage of the always-on, asynchronous, and public
qualities of networked communication to pool knowledge in a decentral-
ized and democratic way. Drawing on the work of Pierre Lévy, Jenkins
observes, "In such a world, everyone knows something, nobody knows
everything, and what any one person knows can be tapped by the group as
a whole" (2009, p. 72). Two features of collective intelligence bear highlighting in relation to distributed mentoring. First, when knowledge is pooled
through collective intelligence, the resulting expertise is greater than any
one individual could offer. Second, collective intelligence has an ad hoc
quality to it; people come together for the purpose of working on a specific
task that interests them and in which they hold some expertise. As a result,
configurations of people are constantly changing depending on the task
at hand.

Many of the new media literacies, such as collective intelligence, are
fundamentally social in nature, highlighting the participatory quality of
online communities that is so central to distributed mentoring. Other
socially oriented skills include networking and negotiation. People skilled
at *networking* have the ability to tap into large-scale social communities and
take advantage of the knowledge sharing that goes on there (Jenkins, 2009).
Because anyone can post anything online, information is abundant and of
varying quality. Skilled networkers are able to identify those people and
communities with the most relevant and valuable knowledge. *Negotiation*
is a necessary skill in an environment where people come together across
geographic and cultural boundaries, bringing with them diverse values and
opinions. Skilled negotiators can take on multiple perspectives and negoti-
ate among conflicting viewpoints. Negotiation can help fanfiction authors
to sift through and distill the conflicting feedback they sometimes receive
in reviews of their stories.

Skills such as multitasking and transmedia navigation are also relevant
to distributed mentoring in fanfiction communities and complement the
skills already discussed. *Multitasking* enables one to shift focus onto the
most salient and useful aspects in an environment (Jenkins, 2009). Skilled
multitaskers know how to navigate a complex and dense informational
landscape by focusing on and shifting attention between the most relevant
details. Such a skill is useful for fanfiction authors who are trying to extract

insight from the many bits of feedback they receive, sometimes through multiple channels. The dispersal of feedback across multiple channels, or modalities, makes *transmedia navigation* another skill that's relevant to the practice of distributed mentoring. Several of the authors we interviewed participated in multiple fanfiction communities, each one with its own set of communication channels (e.g., forum posts, private messaging, commenting on stories). They had to become adept at scanning these multiple modalities for feedback relevant to their immediate writing objectives.

Collectively, the new media literacies described here call attention to the qualities of networked technologies and how they shape social practices in online communities. We turn now to an enumeration of the seven attributes of distributed mentoring, each of which depends on and leverages the qualities of networked technologies. In short, without networked technologies, there would be no distributed mentoring.

Seven Attributes of Distributed Mentoring

In our work, we identify seven attributes that operationalize and describe the process of distributed mentoring. These attributes are: *abundance, aggregation, accretion, acceleration, availability, asynchronicity,* and *affect* (Campbell et al., 2016). In this and further research, we have found evidence of all seven attributes across multiple fandoms and platforms. These seven attributes are not completely independent but rather are intertwined, affecting and resonating with one another throughout the mentoring process. Nevertheless, in this section we focus upon each attribute in turn, describing it in detail and providing multiple examples.

Abundance

Perhaps the most noticeable characteristic of online, distributed mentoring that we observed on Fanfiction.net is the sheer volume of review responses. This volume is enabled by networked technologies that connect thousands of people across the globe and allow them to create and share content around the clock. The archivable and searchable quality of this digital content also contributes to the abundance of review responses.

By itself, a single comment on a story, such as "loved it," is relatively meaningless. But if a writer receives dozens or hundreds of similar comments, the simple presence of positive feedback in these quantities offers valuable guidance to the author: "I've received literally thousands of positive reviews and some truly wonderful letters and messages from people who have been genuinely touched by my writing, and it's been a massive confidence boost that helped me get through university without quitting and still helps me today if I'm feeling down" (Author 9, *Harry Potter*). The mere presence of a large number of shallow positive reviews can indicate to authors that they have done something well in their fanfiction writing.

Additionally, authors repeatedly stated that the amount of feedback they received from others was an important reason why fanfiction was a superb training ground for anyone who hoped to produce original fiction in the future. One published author who started out writing fanfiction noted in a blog post that she received more comments in a single week on her fanfiction writing than she had in multiple years on her original fiction.

Aggregation

Taking advantage of the collective intelligence enabled by networked technologies (Jenkins, 2009), authors participating in fanfiction communities receive mentoring from many distinct sources. Based on our interview study and ethnographic observations, we noted that authors collected multiple small pieces of advice in a variety of forms, including story reviews, discussion forum responses, and Skype chats. Making use of transmedia navigation (Jenkins, 2009), authors compiled these disparate forms of digital feedback across platforms and modalities. These small bits of mentoring were aggregated, as in distributed cognition (Hutchins, 1995; Jenkins, 2009), creating a whole greater than the sum of its parts. Individual pieces of feedback may not be sufficient in either depth or quality to be considered mentoring on their own. However, taken in the aggregate, authors are finding mentorship from the fanfiction community as a whole: "I can't think of any one person [in particular who has influenced me], I take inspiration from a number of people" (Author 10, *My Little Pony*). Networked publics and online connections, which provide multiple channels of feedback and mentoring, such as private messaging, author's notes, reviews, and Skype chats, contribute to a rich fabric of aggregation and increase the effectiveness of distributed mentoring: "If I've got an idea, but need to spin it out a bit more, I'll just pop into one of my 30+ member Skype chats and toss it out there. I can always expect good feedback there" (Author 13, *My Little Pony*).

In addition to receiving feedback from various channels, an author may collect reviews from many unique individuals, which often provide a variety of viewpoints on a single piece of writing. We found that an author who receives ten reviews on a chapter will most likely receive five targeted pieces of feedback plus several other encouraging remarks. This aggregated commentary provides authors with significant feedback on the strengths and weaknesses of their writing.

Accretion

One characteristic particularly facilitated by networked publics is the ability of mentors to interact with one another as well as with their mentees. We discovered that this interaction occurred on multiple fanfiction sites in a persistent, cumulative fashion, thus enabling an accretion of knowledge that facilitated authors' learning process.

For example, FIMfiction.net provides user groups and associated forums, which many of the authors we interviewed found helpful as writing resources. Members often posted on these forums to seek advice with their writing problems, such as characterization or grammar. These publicly accessible forums enabled any group member to reply to any post. At times, respondents simply offered direct advice to the original poster, but in other cases, members would reply to others' responses as part of an ongoing conversation. They might contradict, agree, or add to others' advice, thus building a more complex and nuanced informal lesson for the original poster.

An excellent example of this accretion of information occurs on one of the FIMfiction.net user groups set up as a "writing school." One author posted a rubric on "how to create an antagonist." In response, over twenty group members posted rubrics of their own, and others contributed additional information and critiqued the posted rubrics. One created a "map of evil" with characteristics of negative traits, noting that not all antagonists have to be purely evil. Another member then responded they would try out this technique with their next antagonist.

This sophisticated mentoring activity pertaining to the creation of an antagonist on FIMfiction.net is a prime example of accretion at work, where the process of developing a fictional antagonist was discussed at length by a group whose members built upon and extended previously posted remarks. (See "Case Study 2: Organized Instruction on FIMfiction.net" in chapter 4 for a more complete description of this forum activity.) Through these distributed postings and exchanges and enabled by the persistent nature of the forum, the information accreted over time. The advice that authors received from this mentoring experience included targeted, cumulatively sophisticated feedback on their writing and detailed answers to their questions.

Acceleration

At times, authors receive conflicting feedback on their work. Although this may at first seem confusing, we found that discussions and conflicts between reviewers lead to more active participation and often yield a more complex and nuanced body of feedback. Reviewers point out holes in one another's arguments or reinforce one another's statements through agreement, cite deep fandom knowledge, and, through the process of argument and conflict, accelerate the process of learning via active discussion. The interconnectedness and always-on nature of online networks particularly facilitated this type of accelerated learning, as we observed participants enthusiastically delving into specialized knowledge of fandom or writing technique, pushing one another to go into more depth in learning about the writing process, and buttressing and reinforcing one another's subtle points of argument.

Another case study from a FIMfiction.net user group that will be described in more depth in chapter 4 ("Case Study 1: Writing Princess Luna") is illustrative of this type of discussion and accelerated learning. In one group, an author asked for advice about writing the character Princess Luna, an antagonist in the first season of *My Little Pony: Friendship Is Magic*. More than twenty members replied, offering helpful suggestions, correcting one another's inaccuracies, and debating differing opinions. This type of discussion and argument enables acceleration of learning, as all participants in the discussion will end up deepening their knowledge. This is a characteristic of distributed mentoring clearly facilitated by networked publics.

Availability

On most fanfiction repositories, such as AO3 and Fanfiction.net, reviews, likes, kudos, and other interactions are publicly visible. The persistent, searchable nature of such communication ensures that commentary is available not just immediately after a story is published but indefinitely, potentially years into the future. This availability in turn facilitates long-term mentoring relationships between authors and reviewers, as illustrated by the following review on Fanfiction.net that implies that the reviewer follows the author with regularity: "The way you craft stories is breathtaking, it really is; you understand the characters better than anyone else I've seen. … Here's to the stories written, and the stories yet to come." Many authors stated in interviews that they replied to all of their reviewers, thus fostering these long-term relationships. The availability of reviews means that authors can learn from their reviewers (and reviewers can learn from one another) for as long as the site is available and they are interested in reading comments, thus further extending the impact of distributed mentoring.

Asynchronicity

The availability of these text interactions in turn allows for asynchronous contributions by any individual, at any time, regardless of location, thus enabling reviewers from multiple time zones to continuously read and reply to other comments. Authors might post a story, go to sleep, and in the morning wake up to multiple thoughtful critiques of their work, which they and other reviewers can then respond to as they wake up in their own time zones.

Asynchronicity across time zones possesses a unique type of power: in Cecilia's previous work, she found that it facilitated online community across multiple types of remote collaborations, ranging from children producing group software on the Scratch learning site from MIT to astrophysicists jointly operating a large telescope remotely (Aragon et al., 2009). Here, we note that asynchronicity adds immediacy, depth, and continuity to the mentoring conversation. It also supports international communication and access to knowledge from across the globe. Thus, asynchronicity is a critical enabling factor for distributed mentoring.

Affect

In interviews, on forums, and in their author's notes, fanfiction writers repeatedly mentioned the positive affect generated by the encouragement and support they received from reviews and feedback. Negative reviews, or flames, were moderated by other reviewers, thus creating a supportive community response. It is vital not to gloss over the emotional aspects of mentoring, particularly for adolescents who are forming their identities and developing self-efficacy. The act of writing, even nonfiction writing, can be an emotionally charged event in which otherwise highly skilled individuals find themselves unable to produce the written communication that is crucial for success in almost every field of endeavor. Authors in these communities cited the emotional support they received as key to their growth as writers. As we noted in chapter 2, scholars have long agreed that psychosocial support such as caring and acceptance is of vital importance to any mentoring process.

Authors continually stated that reviews are a crucial source of motivation for them and that receiving encouraging reviews helps them persevere in developing their writing ability. Over and over again, writers cited the personal satisfaction that comes from participating in the community: writing fanfiction, having others read it, and in turn reading and commenting on others' writing. Producing good, clear written communication is an important skill in today's world, and it often requires substantial effort to do well. Without an affective component or element of enjoyment driving the desire to produce high-quality writing, it can be difficult for anyone to persevere in such a learning challenge. The cumulative inspiration that comes from receiving comments and reviews on their writing may also encourage authors to mentor others. More than one author we interviewed noted that they wrote reviews because they were all too aware of their importance. Author 6 (*Doctor Who*) stated, "I make it an effort to review everything I read. ... I know how much reviews are appreciated on this site."

In our analysis of 177 million reviews on Fanfiction.net, as well as our ethnographic study and surveys of other fanfiction repositories, including AO3, LiveJournal, FIMfiction.net, Whofic.com, and others, we found that reviews were overwhelmingly positive and supportive rather than negative. Our observations suggest that shared affection for the fandom generates a sense of community and kinship and contributes to the positive atmosphere. In the relatively rare instances when negative reviews were posted, we witnessed community members come to the defense of the author. One controversial *Doctor Who* story received a few flame reviews, but many more were comments supporting the author, such as this one: "Just ignore the stupid [person] who is leaving those horrid reviews. She can take all her stuffy little remarks and shove them where the light don't shine. This is a fantastic story, I just had a shitty day and this story has really helped me smile." Thus the review system in this community tends to self-correct in the direction of positive affect. The ability of reviewers to interact with one another enables this type of positive emotional resonance among the group and facilitates a supportive community. The effect of a supportive environment should not be underestimated when it comes to facilitating mentoring and learning.

How the Attributes Work Together

The seven attributes of distributed mentoring are interwoven and support one another. As participants view others' responses (availability), they take these perspectives into account when creating their own responses or reviews (accretion) and then can contradict or support other respondents (acceleration). As stories increase in their number of reviews (abundance), we observed a concomitant increase in the amount of discussion present in these reviews (accretion), suggesting that exchanges in distributed mentoring become richer and more complex as the number of participants increases (aggregation). The persistent nature (availability) of computer-mediated communication (CMC) makes it possible for authors to consider multiple voices together, both in the present and in the future, thereby supporting the attributes of aggregation, accretion, acceleration, and asynchronicity. This may be challenging in non-CMC contexts, where human memory limits the number of responses a person can remember. In addition, the public nature of communicating in networked environments such as fanfiction sites allows for a high level of interaction among reviewers, who can react to and build on one another's comments asynchronously and over the long term. This quality of networked communication supports the attributes of abundance, accretion, acceleration, availability, and affect. In contrast, traditional ideas of mentoring are grounded primarily in one-to-one relationships, which are easier to maintain in the physical world. Mentoring facilitated by the internet can move past the limitations of the physical world to allow numerous mentors to engage one another on the same topic asynchronously when providing advice to mentees.

The Broader Significance of Distributed Mentoring

Understanding in more depth exactly how networked publics facilitate this novel type of mentoring has the potential for large-scale impact on both formal and informal learning. Clearly, a great deal of knowledge formation, learning, and discovery are taking place online, and young people are creating new ways to learn from and teach one another. The seven attributes of distributed mentoring provide useful scaffolding to begin to understand these new processes of teaching and learning.

In the next two chapters, we employ these attributes to go both deep and wide to explore distributed mentoring in fanfiction communities. In chapter 4, we explain why and how we conducted our ethnographic study of Fanfiction.net and FIMfiction.net. In chapter 5, we discuss how we came to utilize data science methodologies to uncover large-scale evidence of distributed mentoring.

4   Our Ethnographic Work in Fanfiction Communities

Why Ethnography?

When we first began this research, our primary goal was to understand the experiences of fanfiction authors from their distinct perspectives as contributing members of fanfiction communities. Because most of us were fanfiction enthusiasts ourselves, we knew from personal experience that there were many ways to participate in these communities and that our individual experiences to date just barely scratched the surface. Therefore, it was important to us that we spend real time learning about the different forms of participation in fanfiction communities, focusing in particular on how young authors interacted with other authors and readers. For this reason, we took an ethnographic approach to the first nine months of our research. We read fanfiction stories and their reviews, observed interactions in writing groups and forums, talked directly to authors, and even tried our hand at writing our own fanfiction.

Ethnography has its roots in anthropology, where the traditional practice typically involved a researcher traveling to and living for several years in a remote, non-Western society in order to study and document the cultural practices of its people. Classic examples from the first half of the twentieth century include Bronisław Malinowski's examination of social institutions in the Trobriand Islands and Margaret Mead's exploration of adolescence in Samoa. Early anthropologists such as Mead and Malinowski immersed themselves in the culture they were studying by learning the native language and participating in daily life alongside the "natives." Through such participant observation, their goal was to arrive at an insider's view of a culture that was previously unknown (at least to Western audiences).

Needless to say, ethnographic work looks quite different today. Although researchers still travel to remote societies, many stay closer to home, conducting their fieldwork in schools (Sims, 2014), libraries (Neuman & Celano, 2012), immigrant communities (Flores, 2015), and even among hackers living in the Bay Area (Coleman, 2012). Even when working in a familiar and nearby location, ethnographers still immerse themselves in the cultures they study, attempting to achieve an insider's perspective on the values, norms, and cultural practices that guide people's daily lives.

Online environments have emerged in the twenty-first century as new sites for ethnographic research (Boellstorff, Nardi, Pearce, & Taylor, 2012). Participant observation in online communities may not involve physical travel to a location (in fact, you need not get out of your pajamas!), but it nevertheless requires researchers to immerse themselves in the cultural practices associated with these communities. As with any offline community, online communities have certain customary practices, norms of behavior, and shared goals and values. Understanding these dimensions of culture requires spending time participating in and closely observing community members and their interactions with one another.

Researchers have applied the tools of ethnographic research to a variety of online environments, such as the emergence of social norms on LambdaMOO (Curtis, 1997), social knowledge construction in *World of Warcraft* discussion forums (Steinkuehler & Duncan, 2008), novice and expert trajectories in a *World of Warcraft* raiding group (Chen, 2012), and players' modifications in Autcraft, a *Minecraft* community for children with autism (Ringland, Wolf, Boyd, Baldwin, & Hayes, 2016). For example, Mark Chen (2012) spent ten months as a participant observer in a forty-person raiding group in *World of Warcraft*. He documented the collaborative practices among the group's members and the processes by which players shifted between experts and novices as conditions changed in the larger gaming community. Kate Ringland's ethnography of Autcraft involved immersive, in-world observations, participating in community activities outside the virtual world, and conducting focus groups in the online forums. This analysis showed how children with autism create and use "mods" to support self-regulation and interactions with others.

We joined this tradition of online ethnographic research to explore mentoring processes in online fanfiction communities. By spending nine months observing and participating in fanfiction communities, we were able to produce "thick descriptions" (Geertz, 1973) of the different forms of mentoring support that fanfiction authors experience when they share their stories on sites such as Fanfiction.net. We talked directly to authors about their mentoring experiences. We read hundreds of stories and thousands of story reviews, as well as discussions in writing groups and forums. To immerse ourselves as fully as possible, members of our research team wrote their own fanfiction stories and received feedback on their writing.

Our research group was composed in such a way that we were able to achieve both an emic and an etic appreciation for our topic of study (Glaser & Strauss, 1967; Miles & Huberman, 1994). By virtue of our prior knowledge of and participation in fan communities, we were able to achieve an insider's (emic) perspective fairly quickly. Almost everyone on our research team was deeply familiar with at least one of the fandoms in our study, and most of us had read fanfiction before starting this work. In fact, only Katie was conspicuously not active in any sort of online fan community prior to our research. Although she made an effort to familiarize herself with the fandoms and sites, she did not immerse herself to the same extent as the other members of the team. This etic stance prompted her to question some of the practices that other members took for granted, helping the group to achieve a deeper, more analytic understanding of what they were observing.

Scoping Our Fandoms and Fan Sites

Our first step was deciding on which fandoms to include in our ethnographic work. This was no small task, as our research team had knowledge of and interest in a variety of fan communities. After much discussion of various candidate fandoms based on books (e.g., *Harry Potter*, *Twilight*, the Sherlock Holmes novels), anime (e.g., *Bleach*, *Naruto*), TV shows (e.g., *Glee*, *Doctor Who*, *My Little Pony: Friendship Is Magic*), and movies (*Star Wars*, *The Hunger Games*), we decided to focus our investigation on three: *Harry Potter*, *My Little Pony: Friendship Is Magic*, and *Doctor Who*.

We based this final selection on a number of factors. First, we agreed that it would be valuable for at least two of us to have deep connections to any one fandom, because fandom knowledge would help us to understand the discussions and stories in the communities. Second, we chose fandoms that were broadly popular beyond our small research group so that the size of and activity within the communities were sufficient for our study. Third, our final selection provided a range of genres (e.g., science fiction, fantasy), media types (e.g., TV shows, books), and length of time in existence. Lastly, we decided to include three fandoms instead of focusing on just one to ensure that whatever dynamics we observed were not unique to a particular fandom.

Once we had chosen our fandoms, our next task was to decide which online communities and platforms should become the primary sites for our research. We faced a broad selection of sites, such as Wattpad, AO3, Tumblr, Commaful, and DeviantArt, among others. Eventually, we agreed that Fanfiction.net, as the world's largest repository of fanfiction and with a primarily young demographic, represented an important site for observing and interacting with fanfiction authors, readers, and their contributions. As of February 2017, more than 1.5 million authors had posted nearly 7 million stories on Fanfiction.net, receiving over 170 million story reviews (Frens, Davis, Lee, Zhang, & Aragon, 2018). Our chosen fandoms are among the most popular on the site. As of February 2019, *Harry Potter* had 801,000 fanfictions, *Doctor Who* had 75,300, and *My Little Pony* had 30,400.

The specific features of the Fanfiction.net platform made it particularly conducive to the investigation of mentoring interactions among writers and readers. We could easily locate and read the cumulative stories of individual writers thanks to the fact that users maintain individual profile pages listing the stories they have authored, along with introductory profile messages and the stories and authors they have marked as favorites. Social features, such as communities, forums, beta-reader listings, and a private messaging system, allowed us to observe and document the different types of feedback that writers receive on their stories.

FIMfiction.net represented our other primary site of data collection. As a single-fandom fanfiction repository, FIMfiction.net allowed us to observe the dynamics in an online community dedicated to just one fandom, *My Little Pony: Friendship Is Magic*. As of February 2019, FIMfiction. net had 251,278 users and 99,448 published stories (FIMfiction.net, 2019). Like Fanfiction.net, members create user pages, although these pages are more customizable than Fanfiction.net profile pages. For instance, members can write blog entries on their pages, leave comments on other members' pages, and create image galleries. Private messaging is another feature that both sites share. We were particularly drawn to a distinctive feature of FIMfiction.net: user groups. Any member can create a group, and topics range from plot development to favorite minor characters. As of February 2, 2019, there were 11,841 groups on FIMfiction.net (FIMfiction.net, 2019).

To help us gain a broader understanding of each of our three fan communities, members of our research team also spent time on the *Doctor Who* fanfiction repository *A Teaspoon and an Open Mind* (Whofic.com), the *My Little Pony: Friendship Is Magic* discussion board Ponychan.net, LiveJournal fanfiction communities, and Reddit.com fanfiction subreddits.

What We Did

We embarked on our ethnography by spending some time reading fanfiction on Fanfiction.net and FIMfiction.net. In addition to acclimating us to our research sites, we were looking out for young authors who had substantial writing experience and were currently actively posting their work in these communities.

Author Interviews

We used our initial author interviews to build rapport with individual fanfiction writers, learn about mentoring relationships, and gain knowledge of and access to fanfiction communities. After the authors agreed to participate in an interview, we sent our questions in three waves via the private messaging systems on Fanfiction.net and FIMfiction.net, waited for responses between the waves, and added follow-up questions to clarify previous discussion points. We continued communicating informally with some of the most helpful participants to gain deeper insight into their mentoring experiences in fanfiction communities.

We specifically targeted participants who were eighteen to twenty-five years old in order to gain insight into how young authors experience mentoring relationships during their formative years. To ensure they had sufficient depth of experience to draw on in their interviews, we verified that all participants had been writing and reviewing fanfiction for more than one year. Before contacting authors, we viewed their user profiles to determine whether they were currently active on the site, how many stories they had published, the dates of their first and most recent stories, and whether they regularly received reviews on their writing. We also used their profile information to infer their likely age range and native language. To facilitate easy communication with our researchers, we reached out to native English speakers only.

Our final sample included twenty-eight fanfiction authors between the ages of thirteen and thirty years, with an average age of twenty-three years. Sixteen of them were members of Fanfiction.net, and twelve were members of FIMfiction.net. Twelve participants wrote *My Little Pony* fanfiction, nine participants wrote *Doctor Who* fiction, and seven participants wrote *Harry Potter* fiction. Because we were mindful of the complex issue of gender binaries and fluidity, which is often the subject of fanfiction stories, we did not require participants to identify their gender. Of those participants who did openly offer a gender identity, nine identified as female (all from Fanfiction.net) and three identified as male (with two from FIMfiction.net and one from Fanfiction.net).

In the first set of questions that we sent to participants, we asked general, introductory questions about why they write fanfiction, how they got started, whether they communicate with other fanfiction authors, and in which fandom communities they participate. We also invited them to ask us any questions they might have. Most participants simply answered our questions, but one author did turn the tables on us after answering the first round of questions:

> **Now, questions for you:** What is your goal here? Just to see how the common man feels about fanfiction, out of pure curiosity, or do you have some specific goal in mind, like trying to stop people from dismissing fanfiction just because it's called fanfiction these days? I can only imagine the looks of people when someone would tell them that, technically, the Aeneid was a fanfiction too, by today's definition (Since Virgil was only trying to immitate/rival [sic] Homer in terms of epics). (Author 1, *Harry Potter*)

This defensiveness of fanfiction writers—and perhaps even wariness of our intentions as researchers—was a common refrain throughout our research. To earn the trust of participants, it was important for us to communicate our research intentions clearly, demonstrate our appreciation for and knowledge of the fandoms we were studying, and become full participants in the communities we studied. To that end, a good portion of our interview transcripts includes off-topic conversation about fandom arcana, as our research team made a concerted effort to communicate their genuine love for fan culture.

In the second and third rounds of interview questions, we delved more deeply into authors' social interactions in fanfiction communities, paying particular attention to their mentoring relationships. We asked them if they left feedback for other authors, where they turned for help with their fanfiction writing, and what kinds of feedback they had received on their fanfiction stories. We also asked if there were authors they particularly admired or tried to emulate and whether they had formed any lasting relationships through their fanfiction writing. In the final set of questions, we asked participants to reflect on whether writing fanfiction had impacted their writing, whether their fanfiction experiences had impacted them more broadly, and whether they would be different in any way if they didn't participate in fanfiction communities.

Fanfiction authors love to write, and so by the end of our interviews we had a lot of data! We started off our analysis by taking stock of what we had gathered. Each researcher read the transcripts of the interviews they had conducted, highlighted comments that stood out to them, and wrote memos reflecting on themes they saw emerging in their batch of interviews. They brought these highlighted excerpts to our weekly team meetings, and we discussed their significance collectively and in relation to our overarching interest in mentoring relationships. Through this process, which drew on a grounded theory approach to qualitative data analysis (Charmaz, 2006; Glaser & Strauss, 1967; Pidgeon & Henwood, 1996), we distilled our themes into a smaller set of overarching themes, which we then used to guide the focus of our nine-month participant observation.

Participant Observation

Members of our research team took on the role of participant observer in the fandom communities with which they were most familiar and engaged. These participant observations, which extended over the course of nine months, allowed us to explore firsthand the themes that surfaced in our author interviews. Because we wrote and published our own fanfiction, our participation also gave us the opportunity to experience mentoring and community dynamics directly.

To avoid any possibility of deception, we introduced ourselves from the beginning as researchers in each fan community that we observed and participated in (Boellstorff et al., 2012). We used our active participation, which included writing our own fanfiction stories, to establish credibility in the community and overcome potential distance between ourselves, as researchers, and community members.

Collectively, we spent ten to twenty hours each week reading stories, story reviews, user profiles, and author's notes on Fanfiction.net. Our participant observations focused on reading the author's notes and reader reviews associated with individual fanfiction stories. Author's notes are a common practice in which authors may ask for specific feedback on their work and sometimes respond to comments they have received in earlier reviews. Reader reviews show up beneath a story (or a chapter of a story) and range from very short words of encouragement to in-depth comments on aspects of the story that the reader liked or disliked. Although reader reviews gave us a good sense of the range of feedback that authors received on their writing, they felt somewhat one-sided because author and reader rarely engaged in an extensive back-and-forth dialogue.

The user groups on FIMfiction.net provided a more interactive and lively environment for our participant observations. We focused our observations on five FIMfiction.net groups that each had between one thousand and five thousand members. All five groups focused on giving and receiving writing help. Three groups were spaces for struggling authors to ask questions, one group was a "school" to help writers learn their craft, and the largest, most active group was a general writing community that allowed questions and discussion. Each week, we spent five to ten hours observing these groups and taking notes and screen captures of what we observed. We also communicated informally via private message with group members to ask them questions about their participation. (These individuals were not part of the formal interviews.)

At the conclusion of our nine months "in the field," we had collectively logged over one thousand hours of participant observation and generated several hundred pages of field notes and memos. As we did with the interviews, we brought our field notes, memos, and initial impressions to our weekly team meetings to discuss themes we saw emerging across our individual observations. We also had our interview themes front and center in our minds (and on the white board), which helped us to focus our discussions. It was during these conversations that we started to take note of the fact that the mentoring we were witnessing appeared to be distributed across participants, platforms, communication channels, geographical locations, and time. Building on our interview analysis and following a similar grounded theory approach (Charmaz, 2006; Glaser & Strauss, 1967; Pidgeon & Henwood, 1996), we ultimately identified seven distinct attributes that capture the full range of mentoring processes that we observed.

Thematic Analysis of Fanfiction Reviews

We came to appreciate the importance of fanfiction reviews through our conversations with fanfiction authors and during the course of writing our own fanfiction stories. The cumulative words of encouragement can be a powerful source of motivation for authors, and the more substantive and specific feedback can help authors improve their writing craft. We therefore decided to investigate reviews on a larger and more systematic scale. We conducted a thematic analysis of 4,500 reader reviews to categorize and quantify the different types of feedback that appeared in reviews posted on Fanfiction.net.

We embarked on this thematic analysis by reading a highly reviewed *Harry Potter* fanfiction story written by one of our interview participants. Each member of our research group read the 133 reviews associated with this story and recorded themes representing the different kinds of feedback offered in them. After discussing this "start list" of codes (Miles & Huberman, 1994) as a group, we shared it with the author to make sure that the themes resonated with how she experienced and interpreted her reviews. In our initial list of codes, we distinguished between reviews that were single words of encouragement (e.g., Amazing!); reviews that offered constructive criticism about some aspect of the writing, such as plot or character development; and posts we considered to be examples of trolling or flaming (these were rare).

We refined our code list by applying it to 777 reviews from six additional *Doctor Who* and *Harry Potter* fanfiction stories. We independently coded these reviews and then came together as a group to discuss areas of disagreement, as well as suggested modifications or additions to our list of codes. In this way, our final set of codes was tied to the themes emerging directly from our data set.

To ensure that we applied our codes consistently and accurately to our corpus of data, we completed four rounds of trial coding. In each round, five researchers independently coded a set of reviews, calculated inter-rater reliability for each code, and then discussed areas of disagreement as a group until we came to consensus (Smagorinsky, 2008). Table 4.1 (excerpted from Evans et al., 2017) shows the codes and their descriptions along with the measure of inter-rater reliability for each code. Each review could have more than one code applied to it, but codes 1, 2, 3, and 4 were mutually exclusive. For all codes except 9, 10, 11, and 13, the Fleiss's Kappa (κ) values were between 0.71 and 0.94, representing excellent agreement (Fleiss et al., 2003). Codes that did not produce excellent agreement occurred very infrequently, which is a common cause for low inter-rater agreement. For these infrequent codes, a second coder checked all reviews that contained one or more of these codes.

Table 4.1
Code name and description, inter-rater reliability statistics (Fleiss's Kappa), code occurrence, and percentage of reviews (total reviews = 4,500) that included each code (Evans et al., 2017, table 1)

	Code	Description	κ	Occurrence	% of Reviews
1	Shallow positive	Positive reviews that do not provide specific feedback about the text.	0.89	1,580 reviews	35.1%
2	Targeted positive	Reviews positively reflecting on specific aspects of the text.	0.79	1,351 reviews	30.0%
3	Targeted corrective or constructive	Critical or neutral feedback on specific aspects of the text, e.g., grammar and plot suggestions.	0.75	747 reviews	16.6%
4	Targeted positive and corrective/ constructive	Both sets of feedback must call out specific aspects of the text described in 2 & 3.	0.72	243 reviews	5.4%
5	Nonconstructive negative	Troll posts or flames where the reviewer is intentionally antagonizing the author.	0.79	45 reviews	1.0%
6	Discussion about the story	Reviewers or authors replying to or referencing each other when discussing the story or starting a discussion by asking questions about the story.	0.94	389 reviews	8.6%
7	Discussion not about the story	Reviewers or authors discussing topics unrelated to the story, e.g., daily life.	0.71	86 reviews	1.9%

Table 4.1 (continued)

	Code	Description	κ	Occurrence	% of Reviews
8	Fandom remarks	Reviewers drawing on canon or fanon (fan canon) to position themselves with regard to their fan knowledge.	0.81	466 reviews	10.4%
9	One-sided connection	Comments suggesting an ongoing relationship on the reader's side, e.g., following the author's collective work.	0.34	175 reviews	3.9%
10	Two-sided connection	Comments suggesting an ongoing relationship between the reader and the author.	0.25	55 reviews	1.2%
11	Review fishing	Reviewers asking for reviews on their own fanfictions.	N/A*	13 reviews	0.3%
12	Update encouragement	Encouraging the author to write more.	0.88	1,240 reviews	27.6%
13	Miscellaneous	Undecipherable text or otherwise uncategorizable.	N/A*	74 reviews	1.6%

*Code did not occur frequently enough to measure.

Once we were satisfied with our list of codes and levels of inter-rater agreement, we had to figure out which story reviews to include in our sample. We were interested in exploring whether popular stories (i.e., stories that received a high number of reviews) elicited the same or different kinds of reviews as less popular stories. To that end, we created three categories of fanfiction stories: high popularity, medium popularity, and low popularity. We noted that the distribution of stories by number of reviews followed a power law, with stories below the 50th percentile having fewer than five reviews on average and stories in the top 0.1th percentile having more than 1,000 reviews on average. With this distribution in mind, our high-popularity category contained fanfiction stories that were in the top 0.5th percentile of stories in terms of total number of reviews. Our medium-popularity category included stories in the 0.5th to 10th percentile range, and our low-popularity category included stories in the 10th to 50th percentile range (stories below the 50th percentile had few to no reviews). Our final data set contained 4,500 reviews sampled randomly from our three fandoms and three popularity categories.

With such a large corpus of reviews, it took us several weeks to apply our list of thirteen codes to the entire data set. When coding was complete, we took a look at which codes were most frequently applied across the data set, as well as within the high-, medium-, and low-popularity fanfiction categories and the three fandoms. To facilitate these comparisons, we converted the total code count into a proportion based on the number of reviews per category. We found no significant differences across the three fandoms and only two notable differences across the high-, medium-, and low-popularity fanfiction categories (discussed later in this chapter). We were also interested in whether certain codes tended to show up together. For instance, perhaps reviewers who followed the author's collective work (code 9: one-sided connection) were also more likely to encourage them to write more (code 12: update encouragement).

What We Found

A Labor of Love

We started all of our interviews by asking authors why they write fanfiction. After all, they're not getting paid; there are no grades; there's not even the satisfaction of personal recognition, as most fanfiction authors use aliases. A clear theme emerged across all authors: for the pure love of it. They love the fandoms, they love writing, and they love exploring their fandoms through creative writing. "I write fanfiction because I enjoy it. Simple answer, but it's the truth" (Author 16, *Harry Potter*). Author 3 (*Harry Potter*) gave a similarly concise, direct answer: "I write fanfiction because it's fun, it's a way to play with characters I love, and because I like writing in general."

Author 4 (*Doctor Who*) connected the fun derived from fanfiction to the ability it gives her to explore her favorite characters on her own terms: "Simplified down to one concise answer? I write fanfiction because it's fun. It's something I can sit down and have fun doing, I can play around in these other worlds and with characters that I LOVE and see what different settings they can be placed in and not worry about it affecting the show/book/movie etc." Author 5 (*Doctor Who*) also reflected on the enjoyment she gets from exploring her fandom's characters in new ways: "I don't think I could pin down any one reason for why I write it—I just enjoy doing it. I love my fandom, and I love taking these characters to new places and putting them into new situations to see how they'll react."

The community of fanfiction authors and readers represents an important dimension of authors' enthusiasm for and commitment to writing fanfiction: "I absolutely love all the fandoms here and the readers; my experience on FFN has been very pleasant. Most people are very polite and kind in their reviews and feedback" (Author 6, *Doctor Who*). Author 3 (*Harry Potter*) stated simply, "It's a nice way to interact with other people who love the same fandoms you do."

Beyond the enjoyment of interacting with like-minded people, some authors identified other fanfiction authors they admired and described how reading their work influenced them. Author 7 (*My Little Pony*) was quick to list nine authors she especially admired on FIMfiction.net. She noted that a particular story written by one of these authors had provided the inspiration for one of her own fanfiction stories. Some authors also spoke about the personal relationships they had developed through their fanfiction participation. Author 8 (*My Little Pony*) stated, "I've made more like-minded friends through FIMfiction than I did in high school. These are people who can almost read my mind with how much they think like me, and I love that."

For Author 9 (*Harry Potter*), her friendship with another fanfiction author was both a personal bond and a source of mutual mentorship. At the time of her interview, Author 9 described how their friendship had begun two or three years earlier when he left a review for one of her *Harry Potter* stories. In the review, he questioned her reasons for a particular decision she had made in the story: "I answered, he replied and it turned into a conversation. Initially we just talked about the fic and about *Harry Potter* in general, but gradually it spread to other books and to our views on various issues that came up in conversation, and it's all snowballed from there until we've become good friends." Author 9 went on to describe how they support each other's writing: "I've published more fanfiction than he has, both number of fics and length of fics, but I wouldn't say one of us has more experience than the other; it's mutual. We ask one another's advice on current fics, and sometimes discuss hypothetical plots that may or may not become fics or original stories someday."

Although these themes were dominant across our interviews, not everyone shared the same perspective. For instance, when asked if she had developed any lasting relationships or could identify other authors whom she particularly admired or tried to emulate, Author 1 (*Harry Potter*) responded,

"Nope, no lasting relationships. Nope, nothing and no one I try to emulate either."

Learning to Write

The authors whom we interviewed unanimously and unequivocally communicated their belief that fanfiction had helped them to hone their craft: "I've learned alot [sic] about writing from my time in the fanfiction world. I've learned some of the rules and a lot of 'what-not-to-do' from reviews and other work" (Author 16, *Harry Potter*). Another author, looking back on the ten years she has spent writing fanfiction, commented, "There's no doubt that between my oldest fics and now I've drastically improved [my writing skills]" (Author 5, *Doctor Who*).

Notably, every author emphasized the support they received from members of the fanfiction community, which they believed contributed directly to their improvement as writers. This help came largely in the form of feedback on individual stories. For instance, Author 10 (*My Little Pony*) indicated that feedback from the fanfiction community was a key factor in becoming a better writer: "Writing fanfiction and getting instant feedback over the past couple of years has improved my writing significantly. I still have a long way to go, but I mostly avoid the standard pitfalls that young writers fall into such as poor flow and sentence construction, flat dialogue, and trivial descriptions."

Similarly, Author 11 (*My Little Pony*) observed that his improvement as a writer was due just as much to the community as it was to the time he invested in practicing his fanfiction writing: "They say every writer has to get passed [sic] a million words of writing before he really starts. My fanfiction has been another step in that road, and the help and advice I've received from others within the community, as well as the writing I've been exposed to in others' works has definitely helped me improve in all sorts of ways."

Author 12 (*My Little Pony*), among others, noted that the learning enrichment within the fanfiction community acted as a supplement to what she perceived to be an insufficient emphasis on writing in formal education: "I have learned many aspects of writing that I either never learned in school or only glossed over (higher-level grammar, poetry, scrutinization of wording and word length). I write slower now, usually because I keep looking back on what I have just written and evaluate it instead of proceeding with my writing."

In addition to helping authors improve their fanfiction, these community-based learning experiences have proved beneficial in other writing contexts. Author 13 (*My Little Pony*) expressed the belief that the experience he gained from participating in fanfiction communities provided him with a significant advantage in his intended college major of creative writing:

> Fanfiction was what got me into writing in the first place. I started in middle school with *Naruto* fanfiction, and now I'm a freshman in a college that approved an application that had been sent in with clippings of my online work. I'm planning on majoring in creative writing—fiction specifically—and more than anything else, fanfiction and the fanfiction community has informed my writing style and ability, and my reviewing/editing abilities. Workshopping with a larger community, which might be an alien experience for many entering my department, is almost a daily routine for me by now.

Even authors who were not pursuing creative writing as a career choice still enjoyed the benefits of fanfiction in other contexts. Author 14 (*My Little Pony*) noted, "I have definitely gotten better at making my papers for college classes more descriptive." These comments suggest that authors experienced significant and generalizable learning benefits from participating in fanfiction communities.

Fanfiction's Broader Impact

Our interviews revealed clearly that the time that authors spend participating in fanfiction communities impacts far more than their writing skills. We've already noted the public hand-wringing about today's young people, who seem to be frittering away their time online, liking friends' selfies and watching cat videos (Bauerlein, 2008). The following quote from Author 13 (*My Little Pony*) paints quite a different picture of what can transpire when youth pursue their passions online: "If not for this fanfiction, I would have never begun writing and would likely never have ended up at the school or place in life where I am now. By picking up fanfiction—which led to a major in Creative Writing—I've likely made a significant impact on the rest of my life." Other authors described similar beliefs that fanfiction had impacted their future direction in life. At the time of his interview, for instance, Author 16 (*Harry Potter*) had already produced an original work of fiction and attributed its existence to the confidence gained from writing fanfiction: "My original novel is due for publication next month. It's a fantasy fiction, part one of a planned four series. If it wasn't for the confidence I got from writing my fanfictions, I would never have even dreamed of self-publishing my own work."

Although Author 16 was the only one to mention having published original work, other authors considered the possibility of authoring original literature after realizing how much they enjoyed writing as a result of fanfiction. The authors viewed fanfiction as a good stepping stone toward original authorship. Author 5 (*Doctor Who*) realized how happy creative writing made her from her experiences with fanfiction and now hopes to pursue original fiction:

> I've always been unsure to whether I'm any good at this writing malarkey or not, but recently I've realised that if I could write books all day I'd be really, really happy. Without fanfiction to train me up I definitely wouldn't have been able to get to this point. Of course, I still think I'm not exactly brilliant and I doubt every word I type, but I think that's sort of just always going to be there. Even two years ago I wouldn't have believed that I could write a book, but now I think I just might be able to.

Notably, authors also learned life lessons beyond writing from participating in fanfiction communities. For some authors, their participation helped them grow personally. For instance, Author 18 (*My Little Pony*) drew a connection between creative thinking and open-mindedness: "If anything, thinking of premises for stories that can fit inside of canon has taught me to think outside of the box and expand things." Author 19 (*My Little Pony*) believed he had not just improved as a writer but as a human being, noting that he was now more tolerant and willing to help others as a result of his community participation:

> I spent over a year heavily invested in writing and reading pony [*My Little Pony: Friendship Is Magic*] fanfiction, and I accomplished some things I'm still quite proud of. That definitely had an impact on who I am. I'm more willing and able to help other writers with their work, I'm less judgemental [*sic*] about fanfiction and a number of other things, and I've certainly learnt a lot about grammar!

Several authors spoke about the emotional support they've received in these communities, which has helped them navigate difficult periods in their lives. Through writing fanfiction and participating in fan communities, they experienced solace and comfort. Author 20 (*Doctor Who*) reflected on why she started writing fanfiction: "Initially, it was an outlet for a depression I was going through. It was theraputic [*sic*]." Author 21 (*Doctor Who*) reflected on the support she received from the community of fanfiction writers and readers, which helped her navigate the stormy years of adolescence:

> I discovered fanfiction five years ago, when I was 15 years old. At that period of my life, I was a struggling teenager that suffered from minor depression, and I was looking for a way of escapism from real life. My love of reading led me to fanfiction, and from then on, I was lost. I first discovered the *Twilight* fanbase (as you know, *Twilight* is one of the biggest communities on here.) This led me to write my first fanfiction piece based on the book series. The reviews and feedback I got was so encouraging—and I met some really nice people. In real life, I was already starting to feel better. Fanfiction saved me. To this day, I am still a great believer in the power of fanfiction.

The Many Forms of Mentoring

Our initial aim in questioning authors about mentoring was to discover formal relationships they had formed with individual fanfiction community members. However, it became clear through our interviews that a traditional dyadic mentor–mentee relationship is just one of many forms of mentoring experienced in online fanfiction communities. When thousands of authors and readers are brought together on platforms that allow for communication across geographic, temporal, and cultural boundaries, the possibilities abound with respect to the types and modes of feedback one can receive. Each individual piece of feedback might be too small to be considered a full-fledged instance of mentoring, but when these pieces are combined— and when they start building on and referencing one another—the result is a powerful form of network-enabled mentoring: distributed mentoring.

Authors received feedback from numerous channels, including fanfiction reviews, FIMfiction.net user groups, beta readers, cowriters, Skype groups, podcasts, Internet Relay Chat (IRC), and other message boards and communities. Through these channels, feedback can be given as a one-to-one, one-to-many, or many-to-one mentoring instance. The experiences of Author 19 (*My Little Pony*) illustrate this variety. In addition to naming the long-term editor of his stories, this author described the many resources that he used to improve his fanfiction and provide feedback to others, which included several message boards as well as a real-time chat client: "I was a regular on the /fic/ boards on Ponychan and MLPChan, as well as the #fic IRC channel on Canternet. I offered feedback for others in the Ponychan review threads, had others give me feedback and editing on my own work, and often participated in discussions about fics and writing competitions."

The message board discussions and chats that Author 19 participated in are spaces where groups of writers and readers can work together to provide advice for other writers. In these venues, previous responses are visible to all participants (*availability*), so contributors can see what has previously been addressed and add their own comments. Inspired by his experience providing assistance through these transient channels, Author 19 created a writing guide for other authors to learn from that is now featured on a popular fanfiction website. He was then able to focus his reviews of particular fanfiction stories on more story-specific issues:

> After doing a lot of individual feedback write ups for authors, I noticed I was spending a lot of time dwelling on the same issues. I'd rephrase the same advice about dialogue punctuation, about show/tell, about all those other basic, general things in just about every review I did. The obvious solution was to compile all that stuff into a general guide, which I could then link to at the top of any review, say "refer to sections X, Y and Z" and then focus my energy on feedback particular to the fic in question.

This writing guide is an example of one-to-many mentoring, where any number of fanfiction authors can benefit from the guide's content, whereas the reviews that Author 19 wrote are an example of a more distributed form of many-to-one mentoring, where a single author can benefit from the input of a diverse set of reader reviews.

The pattern of working with public, group mentoring resources as well as private, individual resources was common among the authors we interviewed. For instance, Author 18 (*My Little Pony*) mentioned having both an individual mentor as well as working with FIMfiction.net groups: "I contact my mentor through private channels, but i do do work for a few groups here. One in particular i use as guinea pigs to test an idea." Author 13 (*My Little Pony*) also participated in FIMfiction.net groups in order to provide assistance, as well as work with other authors one-on-one: "I'm a member of several reviewing groups and I routinely work with new authors to help them improve their stories. I've also personally tutored at least three or four writers in improving their work, and I'm a prereader/editor for a fair few of my friends."

Whereas Author 18 discussed using reviewing groups to test out her ideas, Author 13 talked about offering feedback on other people's stories. Together, these comments point to the reciprocal nature of mentoring experiences in online fanfiction communities. Author 5 (*Doctor Who*) addressed this reciprocity explicitly when she discussed how the mentoring she received inspired her to provide similar support for a new writer:

> I'll just add to the mentoring point—it's sort of come full cycle for me. When the girl PM'd [private messaged] me asking for advice, I did realise that I used to be her. Back in the day I wrote so badly that people flaming and trolling me would've been perfectly viable. Luckily I had people to push me up and advise me to turn me into the author I am today, so I found it really important to do exactly the same for her.

This quote also touches on the positive, supportive environment that Author 17 experienced through her fanfiction writing experiences, which emerged as another important theme in our research (affect). Similarly, Author 22 (*My Little Pony*) recalled his experience as a beginning author as motivation to write story reviews:

> I usually search for beginning authors and leave tips on how to improve. Such as better pacing, less telling, and most of all, trying to tone down a Mary Sue [self-insertion] type character or red and black alicorn OC [original characters]. What prompts me to leave feedback is that I used to be as inexperienced or beginning as a newbie on the site just like them not too long ago, so if I can help in any way, I'm going to try my hardest.

FIMfiction.net Case Studies

During the course of our participant observations, one member of our research team (Julie) spent about two hours each week in various writing groups on FIMfiction.net. She became intrigued by the mentoring processes taking place in two groups, particularly as we were formulating our ideas about distributed mentoring. She decided to focus the next several months of her observations on these two communities in order to help our team gain an in-depth understanding of specific instances of distributed mentoring. These case studies provided a nice complement to our broader analysis of story reviews on Fanfiction.net, described below.

Julie was the perfect person to conduct these observations. She had extensive knowledge of the *My Little Pony* fandom and had posted her own fanfiction stories on FIMfiction.net. She was therefore well positioned to engage in the writing group and interpret the interactions she observed. She shared her observations and impressions with the rest of the team in our weekly meetings, and together we identified notable posts, comments, and interactions among community members (Heath & Street, 2008; Merriam, 2009; Smagorinsky, 2008). The posts shared here were particularly generative discussions that we all agreed exemplified the seven attributes of distributed mentoring.

Case Study 1: Writing Princess Luna

The first case study was a general writing community that represented the largest, most active writing group on FIMfiction.net.[1] In this group, authors ask for advice about specific aspects of their writing, such as plot progression or the development of new relationships (or "shipping") between two characters. This group stood out to Julie as a particularly active group with lively conversations, and she was interested in investigating it in greater depth.

We selected one such lively conversation as being representative of many of the question-and-answer posts from this writing group. The original poster was seeking guidance on how to write the character Princess Luna, who is an antagonist from the first season of *My Little Pony: Friendship Is Magic*. The post received forty-six responses from twenty different respondents (availability). Figure 4.1 illustrates the direction of responses in this post. A larger arrow size indicates multiple responses in that direction. This figure shows that the majority of respondents (twelve total) replied to at least one other respondent who was not the original poster (accretion). Two of these respondents didn't reply to the original poster at all and instead directed their comments only to the other respondents. The remaining eight respondents replied directly to the original poster without interacting with the other respondents.

As respondents engaged directly with one another, they sometimes corrected one another (acceleration), as when Respondent 5 mistakenly said that Luna spoke Old English. Respondent 6 replied, "It's important to note that Luna doesn't speak in Old English. We wouldn't be able to understand anything she says otherwise." Other times, respondents built on the advice

---

1 We first presented this case study in Evans et al. (2017).

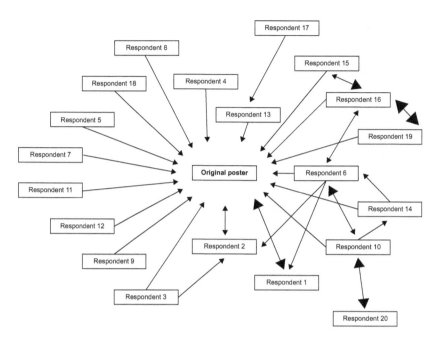

Figure 4.1
Map of forum responses.

of a previous respondent. For instance, Respondent 1 suggested, "From the limited amount of stories that I have read, Luna is usually portrayed as a gamer or somewhat out of touch with modern culture." Respondent 6 replied in agreement: "While I'm picky about the kind of technology that I would introduce into a story, Luna being behind the times is right on the money."

At one point, Respondent 16 and Respondent 19 started to debate when different forms of speech were appropriate for Luna based on her backstory as a character (acceleration). The debate, excerpted below, reveals the depth of fandom knowledge that these respondents possessed, as well as how they were able to disagree with each other in a respectful way (affect).

Respondent 19: [Original Poster] honestly, Luna doesn't even talk in that voice at this point.

Respondent 16: [Respondent 19] She said it's going to take place before her banishment.

Respondent 19: [Respondent 16] We already saw that she talked in her normal voice before the banishment

Respondent 16: [Respondent 19] Unless her alter-ego was already in the driver's seat there. She always spoke "normally."

Respondent 19: [Respondent 16] yes, so why change it?

Respondent 16: [Respondent 19] Just because her alter-ego, a potential outside possessor spoke normally, doesn't mean Luna did? Conversely, obviously Luna spoke like that at least some of the time, when she was being formal. It might have been following out of favor colloquially. But you would still need formal speech for a fic with Luna as a real Princess. You're bound to run into it either way.

Respondent 19: [Respondent 16] She talked normally before she was changed into her alter-ego did you see the video?

Respondent 16: [Respondent 19] Yup. Watched it all the way through, since it remains awesome. But as I said, just because Luna turned into her alter-ego after that physically, doesn't mean she wasn't already in control mentally.

Respondent 19: [Respondent 16] I guess, or maybe the writers were just lazy

Respondent 16: [Respondent 19] It's a pretty good explanation for most anything.

Respondent 19: [Respondent 16] yep

This debate illustrates how the public forums on FIMfiction.net provide a context for participants to build on one another's opinions as well as to disagree (accretion, acceleration). In her back-channel conversations with authors, Julie asked them how they use the diverse pieces of feedback they receive through conversations such as these. How do they make sense of divergent opinions? How do they prioritize advice? Julie's informants discussed a variety of strategies, from trying all advice and judging what works best ("I guess you could say I mix the advice. I try each solution one at a time to see what works and what doesn't.") to combining different pieces of advice that point them in a particular direction ("I usually just look through the responses and pick whichever ones seem to work best for me. This does mean that I will often compile ideas from various people, and so far it's worked very nicely") (aggregation, availability).

Case Study 2: Organized Instruction on FIMfiction.net

The second case focused on a user group set up as a writing school to train new authors about different aspects of the writing craft. The school's mission statement indicates that the goals of the group are to "gather together our collective knowledge on writing stories, provide a secure, functional environment to hold this knowledge, and distribute this knowledge to as many users as we can." We interviewed the creator of this group, and he stated that after reading poorly written fanfiction stories, he was inspired to start a group to supplement what he viewed to be insufficient instruction on writing in the American educational system. He recruited more experienced authors to act as "professors" for the group and provide instruction for beginning authors.

On the group's forum, the professors can post lectures and activities on their topics of expertise (availability). These posts are followed by discussion among the group's members, where less experienced authors can ask for clarification and participate in writing exercises (accretion). Additionally, other more experienced authors will often step in and contribute additional advice on the topic of instruction, debate with the original poster about the topic, and provide assistance to the less experienced authors (acceleration). Because of these contributions, what was originally a one-to-many mentoring experience becomes a more collective experience.

One such instructional post by a professor consisted of an activity for developing an antagonist in one's story. The professor explained that creating an antagonist requires a different system from the one used for creating other characters. In this post, the professor included the following rubric for creating an antagonist, along with an example of a filled-out rubric:

Name:
Species/Outline of Concept:
Age/Date of Creation:
Appearance:
Personality and Traits:
Goal or Directive:
How They Feel about the Protagonist:
Response to More Powerful or Authoritarian Entities:
Strengths over Protagonist:
Weaknesses:

Twenty-one group members posted completed rubrics, and four members contributed additional information on the topic and commented on others' rubrics (availability, asynchronicity). Respondent B added to the exercise by providing a map of evil, with different categories and characteristics of evil traits; however, Respondent B also left a caveat stating that "not all antagonists have to be evil. In fact, making your reader sympathize with an antagonist is an advanced narrative technique." To this comment Respondent A, who had previously posted a completed rubric, replied, "Funny you should mention this. I plan to try this out with my next antagonist. With my current antagonist, I developed him so that the readers absolutely despise him. Which is actually not that hard to do."[2] This reply indicated that Respondent A valued and agreed with the advice that Respondent B had contributed to the conversation (acceleration, affect).

Respondent F created a unique conceptual antagonist described as "negative energy that can drive anyone it interacts with to insanity." Respondent I stepped in and replied with detailed advice on how to flesh out Respondent F's antagonist:

> Only appearing in dreams and feeding off of the "insanity" of its victims, presents a logical fallacy if you want to state that this antagonist existed at the beginning of the universe. Depending on how you view your world's creation, there might not be anything for the antagonist to do until intelligent life comes about. I would avoid having to delve deeply into history and back-story by making the antagonist's inception more recent.
>
> The "negative energy" that makes up the entity should have a physical aspect. A wisp of animate smoke or the quintessential radiation from an object (for example a magical virus or the like). Doing this gives the concept a focus, and prevents the story from becoming a total mind game.
>
> You should really decide once and for all if this entity has sentience or not (are its movements instinctual, or is it simply a mindless zone of insanity?) This does not necessarily have anything to do with insanity, and I suggest you choose one or the other. If you choose to have it show your worst fears, it should probably feed on something other than insanity, like fear.

These examples of respondents building on the original post topic and stepping in to provide assistance to less experienced writers show how the instruction occurring in these lectures and activities is a collaborative, distributed effort. FIMfiction.net groups provided numerous instances of this type of mentoring.

---

2 Quotes are modified to protect the privacy of the respondents.

Documenting Distributed Mentoring through Fanfiction Reviews

Our interviews and participant observations underscored the central role that story reviews played in authors' mentoring experiences in fanfiction communities. Author 6 (*Doctor Who*) explained that she had written hundreds of reviews because she knows how important they are: "According to my General User Stats page, I've submitted 796 reviews on FFN dot net. I usually leave reviews for stories I really enjoy, or for stories I find don't have many reviews. I make it an effort to review everything I read. ... I know how much reviews are appreciated on this site." Story reviews were extremely valuable from a research perspective as well, because they provided a public, persistent record of how small pieces of feedback can collectively work together to provide direction and encouragement to authors. Therefore, they presented a great opportunity for our research team to document the patterns and prevalence of distributed mentoring in a more systematic way once we felt we understood the phenomenon from the perspective of authors (and we include ourselves as authors!).

As anyone who has ever read the comments underneath a Facebook or Instagram post might expect, the single most frequently occurring code (35.1 percent of reviews) was for shallow positive comments, such as "Awesome story!" and "Incredible." In addition to giving authors an emotional boost (affect), these reviews can collectively signal to authors that their story is moving in a promising direction (aggregation, abundance). Another frequently occurring code—update encouragement, occurring in 27.6 percent of reviews—also serves a motivating function for authors to keep moving forward with their stories (affect).

We were interested to discover that when we looked at all instances of substantive, targeted feedback together—including purely positive comments, constructive criticism, and a mixture of positive comments and critiques—these kinds of feedback occurred in more than 50 percent of the reviews. This means that a substantial portion of reviews are going beyond a simple thumbs-up response and engaging with specific aspects of a given story (aggregation). Author 9 (*Harry Potter*) reflected on the value she derived from both shallow positive and more substantive, targeted reviews: "The brief positive reviews probably make up the majority, and I don't tend to dwell on them very much, though obviously they're very nice reviews to receive. The more specific ones make a little more of an impact, they usually refer to something I was particularly pleased with or something I felt was harder to convey."

Consistent with the culture of reciprocity we discussed previously, review fishing was the least common code, showing up only thirteen times in our data set of 4,500 reviews. Also consistent with our interview and participant observation findings, we found very few examples of nonconstructive negative comments (affect). Only 1.0 percent of reviews contained comments such as flames (e.g., "I never thought that human spawn could create such a horrible piece of crap"). In fact, it was more common for reviewers to come to the defense of authors who received such flames. For instance, one controversial fanfiction story written for *Doctor Who* contained an unusually high proportion of flame reviews. However, it received an even greater number of reviews defending the author, such as the following: "Do you realise what you've started? It's like a war between all of the fans who hate Reinnette [*sic*] or enjoy this story and those who have their heads stuck up their butts and have nothing better to do than be rude about this fic. Quite frankly screw them, and good for you, because I think you're going to go down in fanfic history for this!"

This low incidence of negative feedback suggests that fanfiction writers are drawn together around a shared love of fandom, a shared desire to keep the story going, and a shared motivation to improve their writing (affect). As evidenced by the frequency of one- and two-sided connections between reviewers and authors (acceleration), participants in these communities are regular contributors, both as writers and reviewers. They are therefore considerably more likely to engage in generative conversation about canon or fanon (10.4 percent of story reviews) or a back-and-forth discussion of the story under review (8.6 percent of story reviews) than they are to flame one another. That said, we are also mindful that the low incidence of flame posts is likely also attributable to the nature of the specific fandoms we focused on in our research (as already noted, there are plenty of examples of negativity in various online fandom communities), as well as the possibility that authors block or delete highly negative feedback.

When we compared how often codes were applied across the high-, medium-, and low-popularity fanfiction categories, we found only two significant differences. As seen in table 4.2, code 6 (discussion about the story) and code 9 (one-sided connection with the author) occurred most frequently in the high-popularity level and least frequently at the low-popularity level. As an example of code 6, readers sometimes responded to the author's notes directly in their reviews. For instance, one author left a note warning readers that they may be unsatisfied with the recent chapter update: "You may find this chapter frustrating. Never fear—the next chapter will be up on Tuesday, and you will have answers." A reader responded to this author's note with the following comment: "You were right. I want to smack both of them. And I have got to say, Hermione better not lose that baby. I want to imagine Severus's face when he finds out lol :)." In contrast, a one-sided connection from reader to author (code 9) might be a post by the reader that indicates they follow the author's work beyond that specific entry (but with no response from the author).

The higher frequencies of these two codes in the high-popularity fanfiction category indicate that authors and reviewers of more popular fanfiction stories are more connected to one another (acceleration). This connectedness echoes the interaction between forum group respondents on FIMfiction.net discussed above. At the same time, our analysis of story reviews on Fanfiction.net uncovered considerably fewer overall instances of a two-sided connection between reader and author (1.2 percent of all stories coded), regardless of popularity category. Based on our participant observations and author interviews, we believe this low frequency to be attributable to the fact that Fanfiction.net members tend to communicate one-on-one through private messaging. In fact, when a Fanfiction.net user clicks the reply icon next to a review, a private message screen opens that includes a quotation of the review. Several of the authors we interviewed stated that they reply to all of the reviews containing constructive criticism using this direct reply option.

Table 4.2

Code comparison across stories that received a high, medium, and low number of reviews (Evans et al., 2017, table 2).

	Code #6 Discussion about the story	Code #9 One-sided connection
χ^2	7.11	8.12
p	0.03	0.02
Percent of high reviews	9.60%	4.84%
Percent of medium reviews	8.27%	3.60%
Percent of low reviews	6.53%	1.60%

Taking Stock and Planning Next Steps

Our interviews uncovered the themes that would ultimately lead us to describe the theory and attributes of distributed mentoring. Through these interviews, we came to appreciate the variety of sources of feedback that fanfiction authors receive and rely on to improve their writing. We experienced the impact of this feedback firsthand as our team members tried their hand at writing their own fanfiction stories. We instantly recognized the experience as one quite distinct from receiving feedback on an essay submitted to a teacher in class. It was even distinct from receiving feedback from a few fellow classmates. One member of our research group commented on the process:

> It's an emotional experience to publish your first piece of fanfiction. I think we were all reluctant, probably even scared, to put that first story out there. It's like putting a piece of yourself on public display. It meant a lot to me to get comments from people who weren't my friends. And it was incredibly validating to know that people all over the world were reading and enjoying something I wrote.

Feedback in fanfiction communities came to us from a variety of people, through a variety of channels, and across geographic and temporal boundaries (availability, asynchronicity). Individually, a single piece of feedback may not be particularly illuminating (though some detailed reviews certainly were), but when combined they formed a richer and ultimately more rewarding sense of how our stories were progressing (aggregation).

Our participant observations and thematic analysis of story reviews allowed us to document the attributes of distributed mentoring in a deep and systematic way. Table 4.3 highlights key examples showing how the seven attributes of distributed mentoring manifested in our case studies of FIMfiction.net and in our review analysis. For instance, accretion was observable in the back-and-forth exchanges between reviewers, who drew upon and built on earlier reviews. Abundance was clearly visible in the large numbers of reviews that many stories receive on Fanfiction.net. Although a single review exclaiming "Incredible!" may not carry much weight, a string of such comments starts to create a strong signal that the author is moving in a promising direction.

As we considered the insights gained from our thematic analysis of a large corpus of story reviews, we became interested in compiling even larger data sets from Fanfiction.net in order to view trends across a broader range

Table 4.3
The seven attributes of distributed mentoring with select examples drawn from our analysis (Evans et al., 2017, table 3).

Attribute	Description	Example from our analysis
Aggregation	In the aggregate, small pieces of feedback from multiple, independent community members help authors to identify strengths and weaknesses in a whole greater than the sum of its parts.	Over 50% of the analyzed reviews went beyond a simple shallow response to offer authors substantive, instrumental feedback on their stories.
Accretion	Reviewers interact with one another, drawing upon and building on earlier reviews.	Reviews containing back-and-forth discussion about the story were found in 8.6% of the analyzed reviews.
Acceleration	Conflict and discussion among reviewers leads to a network of feedback embedded with rich knowledge about the fandom and writing.	Our case studies of FIMFiction.net showed how participants interacted with one another by correcting inaccurate information, supporting useful suggestions, and debating differing opinions.
Abundance	The large number of reviews can increase the weight of even the shallowest of feedback.	Both the thematic analysis and the case studies showed the large amount of feedback that participants exchanged on Fanfiction.net and FIMFiction.net.
Availability	Online text-based communication between authors and reviewers remains available long into the future, allowing participants and observers to continue to learn from these exchanges even after they become inactive.	Our case studies showed how the public nature of the forum posts on FIMFiction.net provided authors with a rich set of (persistent) advice to inform their stories.
Asynchronicity	The asynchronous nature of online text-based communication allows diverse authors and reviewers to engage in discussion even when synchronous collaboration would be impossible.	Our case studies of FIMFiction.net showed how participants responded to one another over time on forum posts.
Affect	Positive comments and interactions provide authors with valuable emotional support and encouragement.	In our thematic analysis, 70.5% of the review feedback was in the form of positive comments.

of authors and reviewers. Our review analysis had comprised a few thousand reviews. But there are many millions of reviews posted on millions of stories written by thousands of authors. What would an analysis of this larger corpus reveal? We also wanted to investigate whether the experience of distributed mentoring contributed to authors' growth as writers over time. Our thematic analysis of story reviews on Fanfiction.net provided evidence of the seven attributes of distributed mentoring, but it did not tell us anything about whether the fanfiction authors' writing was actually improving through their participation in fanfiction communities. We turn to these questions in the next chapter.

5   The Data Science of Fanfiction, Learning, and Writing

Why Human-Centered Data Science?

After spending nearly a year immersing ourselves in an ethnography of fanfiction and distributed mentoring, we decided to extend our gaze beyond the initial focus on three fandoms. After all, we were studying a massive and varied phenomenon. Fanfiction.net hosts over ten thousand fandoms, and we had already noticed differences in style and ethos from community to community. Certain topics were avoided in one fandom yet extremely popular in others. We'd also observed differing demographics from fandom to fandom.

Nevertheless, we had obtained clear qualitative evidence for the existence of distributed mentoring across our three fandoms. Had we discovered a broader general phenomenon, or was it limited in scope? Would it be possible to find quantitative evidence for distributed mentoring having an effect on authors' writing? In other words, could we scale up our qualitative findings to the vast extent of online fanfiction on Fanfiction.net?

Our problem was not unique. Researchers attempting to study phenomena involving social media, or any type of human-generated text data sets, have often found themselves stymied. They can apply natural language processing or other automated techniques to immense quantities of text, only to find that the results, though potentially interesting, are fraught with misunderstandings, lack of subtlety, ethical concerns, or absence of vital depth. Alternatively, ethnographers, sociologists, or other qualitative researchers can utilize well-tested and sensitive techniques to explore these fascinating data sets up close, only to wonder if they have perceived only a small portion of the whole, which may not be representative. The resulting conundrum means that researchers are forced to sacrifice either breadth or depth in their analysis, as it is simply not possible to manually analyze the staggering quantities of human-generated data that are being released into the world today. (To select only two of the many text-based channels available to people today, texting and Twitter, Domo [2017] estimated that 15 million texts and 456,000 tweets were generated per minute in 2017.)

The data science of text—often defined as computational and statistical techniques carried out upon text data, including natural language processing, machine learning, and other statistical and automated procedures—promises to address some of the issues of scale. Nevertheless, human-generated text is subtle and various, and despite the allure of data science, simply possessing enough data and a powerful computational cloud isn't sufficient to resolve even some of the more visible issues, such as machine translation of text from one language to another, let alone any deeper concerns. The field of digital humanities, which both applies computational approaches to study research questions in the humanities and examines how the use of digital technology for humanities changes the environment of study, has been fraught with controversy related to such challenges (Dinsman, 2016; Svensson, 2010). It seems clear that qualitative techniques, textual analysis, ethnographic understanding, and more human-centered approaches must be used in combination with the data science of text to grapple with the immensity of social media and human text communication.

But it's not obvious how best to combine and merge these two very disparate approaches to understanding our world. Human-centered data science, an emerging field at the intersection of human–computer interaction, computer-supported cooperative work, and data science, attempts to gain insight into the complex interactions among individuals, groups, society, and technology that are being catalyzed by the explosion of data that characterizes the contemporary world. In this chapter, we describe our research in human-centered data science as applied to the study of distributed mentoring and fanfiction. We also show how human-focused explorations into the blending of quantitative and qualitative techniques over large text data sets can be illustrative and successful at the same time as they expose opportunities for deeper thought and reflection about ethical issues, societal trends, and educational and cultural theories and for a more profound appreciation of how young people are shaping and being shaped by today's new technologies.

Our Process

For the reasons listed above, after concluding our ethnographic work, our research group decided to take a step back from the in-close observation of individual fanfiction authors and readers that we explored in chapter 4 and use our qualitative findings to guide a computational, quantitative approach to studying how distributed mentoring appears and is utilized in fanfiction communities. We knew from our ethnographic study that there was no "one size fits all" approach to fanfiction because the communities that have sprung up among various source media have each developed their own internal processes and guidelines, their own conventional wisdom applied within each community. We sought to gain breadth in our understanding of the phenomenon of distributed mentoring, while keeping in mind ethical precepts and the desire to avoid overgeneralization or lack of subtlety in exploring these rich and varied productions of fiction.

In recent years, large-scale data collection and analysis have been opening new frontiers for understanding societal trends in learning and writing, including those that may be found in fanfiction repositories. In 2016, Smitha Milli and David Bamman applied computational methods to study fanfiction communities as both large-scale literary archives and social networking platforms. They proposed using fanfiction communities to predict reader responses in the serially published literary market (Milli & Bamman, 2016). This type of computational analysis of large-scale human-generated text data is likely to become ever more popular as advances in statistical machine learning and other data science techniques continue to improve our understanding of text corpora too large for human-scale qualitative analysis.

In February 2017, our research group collected 61.5 billion words of fiction and over 6 billion words of story reviews from Fanfiction.net. We chose to focus on Fanfiction.net due to its younger demographic (Alexa, 2017), because we were studying distributed mentoring in young people and not fandom in general. Our data set included 672.8 GB of data, comprising 6,828,943 stories, 8,492,507 users, and 176,715,206 reviews. Our goal was to collect and analyze the data via human-centered data science methods, combine them with the in-depth ethnography described in chapter 4, and thus obtain a broader understanding of the nature of distributed mentoring as it occurs among young people writing fanfiction and posting on Fanfiction.net. We believed that our synthesis of data science, interactive visualization, and qualitative analysis would support the theory of distributed mentoring and present evidence of improved skills influenced by community participation.

Measuring learning is always difficult and controversial, especially in informal settings. With vast text data sets such as the one from Fanfiction.net, an additional problem is the inability of researchers to manually examine the data within a human lifetime. To gauge the presence of mentoring and learning, our research group relied on human-centered data science and refrained from drawing conclusions based purely on automated analysis. Instead, we looked for measures that have been shown to capture specific elements of learning in written text. However, we acknowledge that no automated measure will be completely accurate when it comes to measuring learning and the ability to write. We do not recommend that automated techniques ever be used as a sole metric for judging learning, as they are easily gamed. Nevertheless, in attempting to understand a data set whose size is nearly beyond human comprehension, automated techniques provide valuable scaffolding. Two such techniques that we found successful were the automated analysis of lexical diversity in story text and sentiment analysis via machine learning of review types. We provide details on our use of these techniques later in this chapter.

In 2017, our research group, led by student Kodlee Yin, collected and published a trove of metadata from the world's largest fanfiction repository (Yin et al., 2017). The following year, PhD student John Frens led other members of our research group including Ruby Davis, Jihyun Lee, and Diana Zhang in expanding the scope of research beyond metadata and into story content and built on our previous work by examining lexical diversity and the outcomes of author-reader relationships (Frens et al., 2018).

In the remainder of this chapter, we start by addressing some ethical concerns regarding fanfiction author privacy, then discuss the processes we used to collect and analyze these enormous data sets, and finally consider the relationship between statistical models, automated processing, and qualitative research.

Ethics and Privacy

One of the important issues we faced when studying this large but often marginalized community was the need to consider the ethics involved and in particular to protect author privacy (Busse & Hellekson, 2012; Fiesler, Morrison, & Bruckman, 2016; Kelley, 2016b; Whiteman, 2012; Zook et al., 2017). As is often the case when exploring potentially transgressive subject matter, fanfiction writers may feel embarrassed about or risk public censure from stories they once felt free to post publicly. To deal with this issue, most fanfiction repositories allow authors the ability to edit or delete stories at any time. In addition, AO3 expressly provides the ability for authors to "orphan" stories they wish to leave posted but detached from their user identities (Fiesler, Morrison, & Bruckman, 2016).

In general, we believe it's important when studying any sensitive population or subject online to take special care to protect privacy. Anonymization of usernames is not sufficient, especially when quoting participants' public posts, as it's extremely easy to type a text string into a search engine and determine exactly who produced that quote. This is why we modified all such posts before quoting them in our publications. In the case of our group's fanfiction metadata release, we chose to exclude story, profile, and review text and only provide metadata (Yin et al., 2017). We also fully anonymized the metadata release via differential privacy (Dwork, 2008, 2011). We wanted to ensure that we were not publicly releasing material that authors had no knowledge of and therefore could not delete at will. This also ensured that we as researchers were not in violation of the EU General Data Protection Regulation implemented in 2018.

Blending Qualitative and Quantitative Research: Metric Selection

In searching for the right type of hybrid approach to use in forming a deep understanding of our data set, we sought to choose a metric that would give us insight into the development of writing in adolescence. Frens suggested the consideration of lexical diversity and led our group in a detailed examination of the properties of this metric (Frens et al., 2018). In this section, we provide the reasons we selected this metric for use in our studies.

Lexical diversity, or the vocabulary range found in an individual text, has been well studied in the fields of linguistics, literacy, and learning. Bates and Goodman (1999) and Durán, Malvern, Richards, and Chipere (2004) have modeled language learning as growth in cumulative vocabulary. Prior research has shown that writing quality as determined by human raters correlates with lexical diversity (Crossley et al., 2011; McNamara, Crossley, & McCarthy, 2010; Yu, 2010). Multiple studies (e.g., Fergadiotis, Wright, & Green, 2015; Jarvis & Daller, 2013; McCarthy & Jarvis, 2010) have identified the Measure of Textual Lexical Diversity (MTLD), developed by Philip M. McCarthy and Scott Jarvis (2010), as an accurate reflection of one aspect of writing quality: the use of a wide range of vocabulary. Based on the number of studies demonstrating a correlation between MTLD and writing quality, our group chose to measure lexical diversity in our fanfiction corpus and correlate it with the abundance and availability of distributed mentoring.

Lexical diversity as a measure of word usage dates back to early quantitative analysis of written text (Johnson, Fairbanks, Mann, & Chotlos, 1944). An early and long-used operationalization of lexical diversity, type–token ratio (TTR), is computed by dividing the number of unique words in a text by the total number of words. Because TTR is correlated with the number of words in the text, it is therefore unsuited to comparing texts of differing lengths (Malvern, Richards, Chipere, & Durán, 2004). Several length-independent measures of lexical diversity have reached wide usage, including D (McKee, Malvern, & Richards, 2000), moving-average type–token ratio (MATTR) (Covington & McFall, 2010), and MTLD (McCarthy & Jarvis, 2010). Our group chose to use MTLD because it outperformed D and MATTR in accounting for lexical diversity independently of other factors and provided a reliable reflection of lexical diversity well suited for narrative discourse (Fergadiotis et al., 2015). MTLD has also been shown to be associated with the quality of written text. McNamara, Crossley, and McCarthy (2010) compared expert evaluations of 120 undergraduate student essays with the lexical diversity of the text. MTLD differed significantly between low- and high-proficiency argumentative essays, with mean scores of 72.64 and 78.71, respectively. The properties of MTLD matched our need for an efficient automated comparison between fanfiction texts of varied length.

MTLD has previously been used as an indicator of language ability and writing ability. Treffers-Daller (2013) evaluated narrative texts written in French by 64 students and found that MTLD of these texts correlated with students' scores on the C-Test, a measure of French language skill.

Olinghouse and Wilson (2013) assessed narrative, persuasive, and informative compositions by 105 fifth-graders and found that their narrative compositions had higher MTLDs. Furthermore, they found MTLD to be more predictive of writing quality in narrative texts than persuasive and informative texts, accounting for 8.4 percent of variance among the narrative texts.

Longitudinal studies have utilized MTLD change in written text as a measure of learning. Mazgutova and Kormos (2015) compared MTLD between argumentative essays written by students before and after an English for Academic Purposes class at a British university and found a considerable postclass increase in MTLD. In one longitudinal study conducted by White (2014), 141 students aged thirteen to eighteen submitted 200- to 1,500-word expository texts written for English class for lexical measures. The mean MTLD increased significantly from grade eleven to grade thirteen of school among New Zealand students aged fifteen to eighteen, demonstrating that a significant period of growth in lexical development occurs in late adolescence.

Thus, any measurement of the potential effects of distributed mentoring would need to control for this late-adolescent lexical development. As we will discuss in depth later in this chapter, we obtained self-reported age data, adjusted by profile date and story publication time, from many of the profiles on Fanfiction.net, and through the use of statistical models, we were able to isolate each of these effects individually. Our research group examined lexical diversity among English-language fanfiction texts by 1.5 million writers and found that scores increased as the writers received reviews, even when the effects of popularity, aging, and practice were controlled (Frens et al., 2018).

Fanfiction.net Data Set and Metadata

Fanfiction.net alone contains enough fiction to fill 615,000 hundred-thousand-word novels. For comparison, Project Gutenberg, one of the internet's largest e-book repositories, has about 53,000 texts in its collection (Project Gutenberg, 2018). Fanfiction.net contains nearly 7 million stories, posted in 28 million chapters, covering over ten thousand fandoms. As of 2017, the average number of chapters in a story was 4.17, with a standard deviation of 8.12 (Frens et al., 2018).

Our research group scraped two snapshots of twenty years of fanfiction data, the first in November 2016, consisting only of metadata (Yin et al., 2017), and the second, more complete data set during January to February 2017 (Frens et al., 2018). The first metadata set, consisting of 10,294 fandoms, was scraped by Kodlee Yin in November 2016, using a combination of Apache HttpComponents and jsoup. We were careful to meter the scraping program so as not to violate Fanfiction.net's terms of service at the time. Group members John Frens and Jihyun Lee later extended the scraping program to collect the full data set and store it in a password-protected MySQL relational database. (See the appendix for details.) The final data set included 672.8 GB of data, with 28,493,311 chapters from 6,828,943 stories, 8,492,507 users, and 176,715,206 reviews.

Fanfiction.net continues to grow rapidly: In the three months from November 2016 to February 2017, we found that almost 22,000 new stories were added and nearly 4,000 new authors joined. More specifically, the data set increased from 6,807,100 stories across 1,516,335 authors in forty-four languages in November 2016 to 6,828,943 stories by 1,520,309 authors by February 2017.

Metadata Public Release

The anonymized metadata set has been released to the public at http://research.fru1t.me (Yin et al., 2017). Variables were aggregated and Laplacian noise added to ensure differential privacy even among outliers (Dwork, 2008; Yin et al., 2017). In order to protect the privacy of the fanfiction authors and preserve their right to delete their work in the future, the full-text data set was not released to the public.

Each row of the November 2016 metadata set contains an anonymized user ID, story ID, and six quantitative and six categorical variables as documented on the release site, including publication date; number of words in the story; number of favorites, followers, and reviews; fandom name and category; language; and content rating. Categories include anime/manga, books, cartoons, comics, games, miscellaneous, movies, plays/musicals, and TV shows. The fandom variable refers to the specific creative product, such as *Harry Potter* or *Twilight*. The stories span 10,294 fandoms and use 46,337 unique story characters 9,308,807 times. Twenty genres (e.g., drama, romance, adventure) were applied to 6,159,491 stories, leaving 647,609 uncategorized.

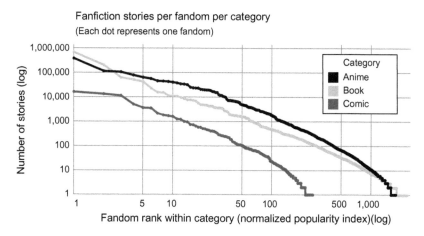

Figure 5.1

An overview of fanfiction story metadata by fandom/category. The books category contains the most popular fandom (*Harry Potter*) by number of stories, but the anime category is much deeper, with multiple fandoms generating more stories. (Image produced by Kodlee Yin.)

We found the largest categories to be anime/manga (1,905,055 stories), TV shows (1,553,815), and books (1,442,290). The most popular genres were romance (3,423,862 stories), humor (1,296,042), and drama (1,147,377). The top three fandoms in November 2016 were *Harry Potter* (713,814 stories), *Naruto* (387,218), and *Twilight* (212,929) (Yin et al., 2017).

We found different "shapes" of fandom popularity within categories (see figure 5.1). Although the books category contains the single most popular fandom (*Harry Potter*) by number of stories, the anime category turns out to be much deeper, with multiple fandoms generating more stories overall.

This work also confirmed previous research that a significant portion of the authors on this site are English-speaking students. We found a marked uptick in posting during the Northern Hemisphere's summer months, with a brief blip in late December (see Yin et al., 2017 for a high-resolution graph of this phenomenon).

Category-aggregated metrics from our study revealed that although anime generates the most stories, fanfics in books and plays received more reviews per story on average. Stories are significantly longer in the books category than they are in any other category (see table 5.1).

Table 5.1

Per category information for the Nov. 2016 fanfiction metadatabase. Note that anime is the most popular overall category, but each anime fanfiction story receives fewer reviews on average than book fanfiction (Yin et al., 2017, table 1).

Category	Stories	Authors	Avg. words	Median words	Words StDev.	Avg. chptrs	Median chptrs	Chptrs StDev.	Avg. reviews	Median reviews	Reviews StDev.
anime	1,876,647	500,902	8,838	2,379	24,639	3.79	1	7.29	24.3	7	93.4
book	1,422,285	488,670	10,009	2,287	27,586	4.56	1	8.32	39.7	7	217.5
cartoon	453,925	138,790	8,885	2,412	25,003	4.23	1	7.28	20.4	7	59.8
comic	52,267	24,924	7,117	1,935	22,021	3.39	1	6.59	12.9	4	52.2
game	634,519	231,497	9,814	2,372	29,887	4.11	1	8.36	14.7	4	91.1
misc.	207,563	101,161	7,544	1,929	37,524	3.83	1	8.26	12.0	3	48.1
movie	291,075	117,251	9,579	2,528	24,178	4.70	1	8.31	23.9	7	77.1
play	60,227	17,958	6,319	2,371	12,908	2.79	1	4.28	41.4	11	132.7
TV	1,404,244	299,347	8,867	2,296	24,040	4.18	1	8.56	23.8	7	79.7

Exploring story length, we found a classic power-law distribution, with a peak at less than one thousand words. Romance contained more stories than any other genre, and Western the least. The most popular combination of genres was humor/romance, comprising 7 percent of all *Harry Potter* stories out of four hundred possible combinations.

As is often the case in data exploration, these findings open up the possibility for intriguing research questions to be answered through further qualitative research (e.g., Why do anime fans produce more stories yet review less? Why do authors write longer works in the books category?). We believe that many more findings remain undiscovered in this enormous metadata set, including differences between fandoms, varying proportions of stories across categories, how genre types differ by language, and many more.

This publicly available metadata set took a substantial amount of time and effort to collect, process, anonymize, and curate. It provides a treasure trove of fanfiction data to explore and is located at http://research.fru1t. me. We hope others can benefit from our efforts, and we encourage all interested parties to download and explore this fascinating data set.

Profile Parsing and Ages

After archiving the metadata set, our group turned to the collection of the full data set, including all story chapters, reviews, and user profiles, and completed this task in February 2017. To find correlations between lexical diversity of fanfiction chapters and the abundance of distributed mentoring in this data set, we had to first separate out all the potentially confounding variables and clean our data. The first variable we examined was author age at the time of writing a fanfiction chapter. Based on our earlier observations and previous research, we believed that the primary contributors to Fanfiction.net were adolescents. Now that we finally had access to the complete data set, one of the first tasks we undertook was to test this hypothesis by parsing all the data and not just a random sample.

Jihyun Lee and members of our research group parsed biography text from the complete set of 8,492,273 user profiles on Fanfiction.net, extracted self-reported age information via regular expressions, and adjusted the ages based on profile update time and story publication date (Frens et al., 2018).

Author age approximations were computed for each fanfiction chapter by adding self-reported age to the difference between story publication date and last user profile update time. For instance, if a user updated their profile in February 2017, listing an age of sixteen years, and then published a story in August 2018, their age at story publication time would be estimated to be 17.5 years.

A total of 284,448 of the user profiles contained self-reported ages. Of these, 72.5 percent fell within the age range of 10 to 20, which indicated that a majority of Fanfiction.net users identified themselves to be in their adolescence. Although there are obvious issues with self-reported data, our findings are supported by data from other sources and previous work (Alexa, 2017; Sendlor, 2011; Yin et al., 2017). A demographic investigation on a random sample of 95,313 public profiles of registered Fanfiction.net members in the year 2010 reported an average age of 15.8, a median age of 15, and a mode of 14 years of age (Sendlor, 2011). According to Alexa's web traffic report, the percentage of users browsing Fanfiction.net from school are greatly overrepresented compared to the internet average (Alexa, 2017). As noted previously, our research group found that the number of stories published by month peaks during the Northern Hemisphere summer vacation and December (Yin et al., 2017). Thus, it's reasonable to conclude that a significant portion of the authors on this site are teenagers in school.

Out of 130,817 users who self-reported gender on their profile page, we found 73 percent of them identified as female and only 11 percent as male. Others have found that fanfiction authors who identify as gender-nonconforming outnumber those who identify as male (Dym & Fiesler, 2018). These findings are supported by multiple sources (Alexa, 2017; Treffers-Daller, 2013), as well our own ethnographic work (Campbell et al., 2016; Evans et al., 2017).

To alleviate the noise generated by self-reported age information, our group removed from consideration self-reported ages that we deemed unreliable, that is, under ten or over ninety-nine. The analysis eliminated 24,792 authors who reported ages that placed their adjusted age below ten. A further 105,184 users were excluded because they did not author any English-language fanfictions, and 21 were removed because their profile update time could not be found.

Largest Sample of Fanfiction Author Ages

The resulting data set included 154,451 authors and their 3,696,107 chapters of fanfiction. This is the largest sample of fanfiction author ages of which we are aware. The average age of authors in this data set was found to be 16.8 years with a standard deviation of 8.3 years. An illustration of all self-reported ages is provided in figure 5.2 below.

To account for the potential covariate of time, we tracked the passage of time between authors' posts. Times for publication of each chapter were not directly accessible on the website but were estimated using related story and review metadata. Each story has a publication date, assumed to be the time of publication for the first chapter. For chapters that had reviews, we used the time of the first review as an estimate of publication date. Chapters with zero reviews were assigned times of publication equal to the nearest known chapter times. An analysis of a random sample of ten thousand stories conducted by group member Jihyun Lee showed that 15 percent of first

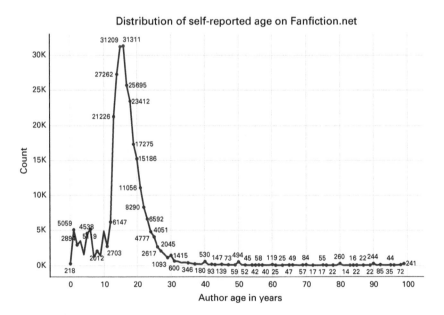

Figure 5.2
Distribution of self-reported age in user profiles. Mean age is 16.8 years and standard deviation is 8.3 years. (Image produced by Jihyun Lee.)

chapters received their first reviews within two hours of publication time, 42 percent within one day, and that the median time from publication to first review was three days. Thus, review publication time is a close proxy for chapter publication time (Frens et al., 2018).

We now go into detail on our methods for scoring lexical diversity, building our statistical models, and extracting the results.

Lexical Diversity Scoring

To compute lexical diversity for each of the chapters in our data set, we selected the Measure of Textual Lexical Diversity (MTLD), developed by Philip M. McCarthy and Scott Jarvis (2010). In an earlier section of this chapter, we explained the reasons why we selected this metric for our research. In this section, we'll discuss the technical features of our algorithm for computing MTLD on our text corpus, including exactly how we calculated a per-chapter lexical diversity score.

MTLD is defined as the average length of substrings within a text that maintain a specified ratio of different words to total words. Computation of MTLD is sequential, starting with the first word in the text and continuing to the end. A running TTR is stored by the algorithm as each word is processed; the running TTR increases as new words occur and decreases with repeated words. The algorithm also maintains a count of "factors," which are defined as sequential groups of words with a TTR of 0.72 or below (McCarthy & Jarvis, 2010). When a factor is found, the running TTR is reset, and the factor count is incremented by one. When the algorithm terminates, any remaining words after the last found factor are used to compute a partial factor, which is 0 if the running TTR is 1.00 and approaches 1 as the running TTR nears 0.72. The 0.72 threshold was calibrated by McCarthy and Jarvis via a corpus of fiction and nonfiction texts (McCarthy & Jarvis, 2010). The output of MTLD is the mean word length of factors within the text.

To illustrate the computation of MTLD, here's an example provided by John Frens on the sentence "I came, I saw, I conquered." The TTR is computed after each word: *I* (TTR = 1.00) *came* (TTR = 1.00), *I* (TTR = 0.66, factors = 1 and reset TTR) *saw* (TTR = 1.00), *I* (TTR = 1.00) *conquered* (TTR = 1.00). In this example, there is 1 factor and a running TTR of 1.00 for a partial factor of 0. The mean factor length is computed by dividing the number of words (6) by the number of factors (1) for an output MTLD of 6.0.

The MTLD output captures lexical diversity independently of the length of the text and is therefore suited for comparing lexical diversity between texts in our data set. John Frens and group members implemented this algorithm in Python and open-sourced the code to make it replicable (see http://www.github.com/jfrens/lexical_diversity). Altogether, we processed 28,493,311 fanfiction chapters with minimum length 100 words and maximum length 610,101 words. A total of 61,560,528,896 words, tokenized by whitespace, were processed.

MTLD scores of fanfiction chapters were normally distributed around a mean of 99.44, with most scores falling between 50 and 150. The minimum score was 2.0, reaching the theoretical minimum output of the MTLD algorithm, and a long tail of high scores ranging from 150 to 2,578,140 yielded a high standard deviation of 486.03.

Although most of the fanfiction chapters that we analyzed received an MTLD score above 50 and below 150, a small but significant number of outliers yielded extremely low or high scores. As is good practice in human-centered data science, we manually reviewed a sample of these outliers. We found that almost all texts with scores below 5 were nonnarrative word repetitions. One author's last chapter consisted of "I LOVE YOU GUYS! HAVE ALL THE COOKIES! (::)(::) (::)(::) (::)(::)," repeating the cookie emoticon for hundreds of lines. We also reviewed a sample of high-scoring texts above MTLD 300 and found that most were nonnarrative, including number sequences, lists of random words, tables of contents, glossaries, random typing, and lists of proper nouns. One author achieved the highest MTLD score in the data set, over 2.5 million, by writing a chapter that quotes a character counting from one to 10,000.

Thus, we eliminated from further analysis 2,678 chapters with MTLDs below 5 or above 300. We also disregarded 22 chapters with erroneous data and 427,662 chapters containing fewer than 100 words (too short to obtain reliable MTLD results). The resulting data set used for our analysis of lexical diversity in English-language fanfiction texts included 53,185,524,320 words contained in 24,835,868 chapters from 5,906,217 stories. MTLD scores of the remaining fanfiction chapters were normally distributed around the mean of 97.35, with a standard deviation of 21.96 (Frens et al., 2018).

The language of each story was obtained from metadata contained on Fanfiction.net. To confirm the accuracy of the language metadata, we algorithmically detected the language using the Python library langdetect. Overall, algorithmic language detection matched the metadata for English versus non-English for 99.5 percent of chapters, above the 99 percent reported accuracy of langdetect. MTLD scores varied significantly with language. Previous studies have used lemmatization with MTLD for non-English languages (Treffers-Daller, 2013). We chose to use only English language texts and did not use lemmatization. Of the total chapters, 25,266,230 out of 28,493,311, or 89 percent, were identified as English based on metadata from Fanfiction.net (Frens et al., 2018).

We now address the statistical analysis of the data, including an explanation for the selection of models, and then present results, limitations, and implications of our work.

Mixed Linear Models and Results

Mixed linear models are a class of regression models well suited to testing within-subjects differences in a longitudinal setting. In a mixed model, fixed effects are used to model continuous independent variables of interest. Random effects are used to account for individual differences (such as differences between students) and group differences (such as differences between classrooms).

We performed regressions on our data set using mixed linear models. Both fixed and random effects were used to model potential confounds while testing the effect of review abundance. For instance, maturation may account for increased lexical diversity in writings while accumulating reviews co-occurs. Thus, a fixed effect was used to model the passage of time. A random effect was used to group data by fandom, as our previous study had found that reviewer engagement varies with fandom (Yin et al., 2017), and MTLD also can vary with fandom.

Figure 5.3 visualizes the relationship between adjusted age and MTLD for English-speaking Fanfiction.net authors who self-reported their ages on their user profiles.

As seen in figure 5.3, the mean chapter MTLD increases from 93.6 at age fifteen to 97.1 at age nineteen and subsequently remains essentially flat. By analyzing the 1,608,824 chapters by 71,983 authors with estimated

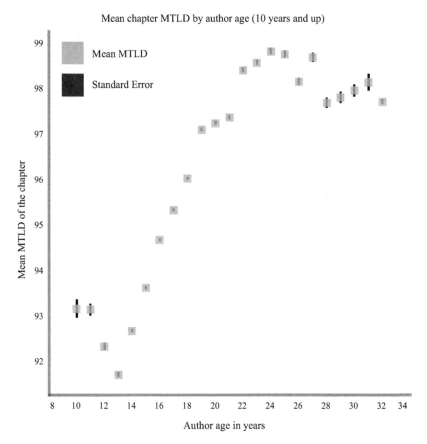

Figure 5.3
The mean MTLD score of chapters, by author age in years, from ten years old and up. Age was adjusted for each chapter based on its estimated time of publication and the user profile update time. 3,696,107 chapters by 154,451 authors are included in the graph. The rightmost point aggregates all chapters by authors aged thirty-two to ninety-nine. (Image produced by Diana Chenyu Zhang.)

ages from fifteen to twenty years old with a mixed linear regression, we confirmed that lexical diversity increases during late adolescence. Age is the only fixed effect; user and fandom are modeled as random effects. The significant ($p < 0.001$) and positive coefficient of 1.66 indicates that each year, MTLD increases during late adolescence. Cohen's f^2 for age was 0.007, indicating the effect size was very small (Frens et al., 2018).

To quantify the abundance of distributed mentoring, for each chapter in the English data set ($N = 24,835,868$), we counted the cumulative number of reviews received previously by the same author. The median number of previous reviews received was 59, and the distribution of cumulative previous reviews among chapters was right skewed (mean = 420.38, standard deviation = 1,741.70), with a maximum of 128,870 previous reviews. To determine if there existed a connection between previous reviews and lexical diversity, we created a visualization with logarithmic buckets of the number of reviews previously received for each chapter and computed the mean MTLD score for chapters in each bucket. Figure 5.4 visualizes mean chapter MTLD score by cumulative previous reviews.

As shown in figure 5.4, the mean MTLD among chapters in each bucket increases as the number of previous reviews increases, from 93.22 with 0 reviews to 102.33 when over 10,000 cumulative reviews have been received (Frens et al., 2018).

We also found that maturation predicts increased lexical diversity, and lexical diversity increases as authors accumulate reviews. We performed a mixed linear regression to examine together the relationship between the dependent variable of MTLD and the independent variables of previous reviews (abundance of distributed mentoring) and days since starting (maturation). This analysis longitudinally tracked MTLD changes during authors' first 50 chapters. We included previous reviews and days passed as fixed effects, whereas fandom and user were random effects. This data set included 16,658,721 chapters by 1,065,606 authors who wrote at least 2 chapters.

The mixed linear model regression revealed that previous reviews and days passed each significantly predicted chapter lexical diversity ($p < 0.001$). For each day of maturation, MTLD increased by 0.0032. For each review received on a previous work, MTLD increased by 0.0018. This analysis

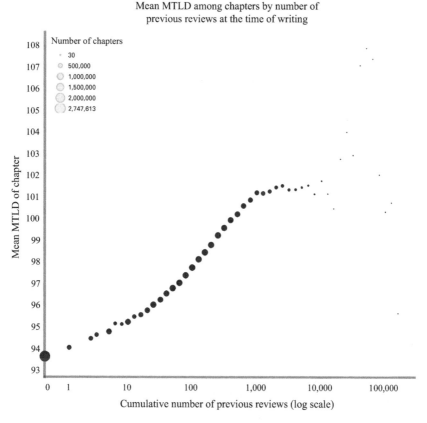

Figure 5.4

The mean MTLD among chapters, categorized by the number of reviews previously received by the author. The x-axis is logarithmic scale. The size of the circles represents the number of chapters in each bucket. (Image produced by Diana Chenyu Zhang.)

aligned with our previous qualitative research (Campbell et al., 2016; Evans et al., 2017), which showed that distributed mentoring uniquely contributes to authors' development. However, effect size as measured by Cohen's f^2 was very small for days and almost negligible for previous reviews (Frens et al., 2018).

To summarize, we found an increase in lexical diversity among fanfiction stories as authors receive an increased abundance of distributed mentoring from others in the community. The improvement is robust when other maturation is accounted for. However, the effect sizes as measured with Cohen's f^2 are small, indicating that much of the variance that occurs in MTLD is not predicted by reviews or maturation. It's not surprising to find this degree of noise in our data, as we are attempting to examine some very subtle constructs. Although our independent variables predict only a modest effect on MTLD, MTLD captures only a single component of the quality of narrative writing, the diversity of words.

A Cautionary Note

A number of limitations need to be considered when interpreting these results. Potentially, there may exist reasons for the lexical diversity increase that are correlated with but unrelated to distributed mentoring, as operationalized by reviews. Our finding obviously also does not imply any causal relationship. To show such a relationship between reviews and lexical diversity, one would need to experimentally manipulate the number of reviews received by the authors. This is a common limitation in the study of informal learning environments, and although we controlled for writers' practice, fandom, and maturation, other needed controls may exist.

Another limitation stems from noise on Fanfiction.net. Some data used in the analysis, such as chapter publication dates, could not be obtained directly from the website and relied on careful estimation based on the associated metadata. To verify that our findings based on estimated chapter times were valid, we ran similar analyses using story publication dates, which are available, and MTLD averages among stories. Parameter estimates for practice, maturation, and previous reviews were statistically significant, positive, and of similar relative size when analyzing by story, which confirmed the validity of our chapter time estimations. An additional source of noise results from the users' capability to modify content after publishing; it's not possible to know the degree to which stories were edited after being published, and one cannot control for the possibility of noise introduced by this capability.

Limitations also arise from assumptions about the associations between our data and particular constructs. Our primary independent variable of review counts measured only one attribute of distributed mentoring, its abundance. However, the number of reviews received by an author does not capture other aspects of distributed mentoring, such as differences in affect, diversity of perspectives, interaction between reviewers, interaction with authors in closed channels outside of reviews (e.g., private messaging, chat, or emails), or mentoring received on sites outside of Fanfiction.net. This constrained measure of distributed mentorship points to an avenue for future work, a deeper examination of the content of reviews. Furthermore, lexical diversity as measured by MTLD does not capture all aspects of narrative writing quality, nor does it represent all learning that occurs among fanfiction writers. This stems from broader issues in both text processing and the study of informal learning: no algorithm evaluates text in exactly the same way as a human, and no behavioral measure can directly view participants' minds to determine what has been learned.

Implications of the Quantitative Analysis

Nevertheless, these findings illuminate the role of distributed mentoring in informal online learning communities and pave the way for future research using similar methods. An interesting finding that resulted from our analysis revealed that accumulating roughly 650 reviews predicts the same increase in lexical diversity as one year of maturation (Frens et al., 2018). Given our analysis of a 61.5-billion-word data set written primarily by adolescents over the past couple of decades, the results underscore the significance of informal learning communities in the lexical development of young adults today, as well as the importance of affordances for distributed mentoring in these communities. The alignment of participation in fanfiction communities with the age range critical for lexical development further underscores the importance of participation in informal writing communities for adolescent learning.

The results of our longitudinal lexical diversity scoring on a large group of authors also reaffirm the efficacy of assessing narrative quality with lexical diversity. The correlation of MTLD increase with practice and maturation align with what we'd expect for a valid, albeit noisy, measure of learning.

Several implications follow from our quantitative analysis of the abundance of distributed mentoring, particularly for members of learning communities such as the fanfiction archive we studied. We found that reviews are predictive of author improvement, especially in the difference between zero reviews and greater than zero reviews. We believe it's important for designers of informal learning communities to encourage participants to provide feedback to newcomers who have not yet received comments on their work. Our previous research indicated that this type of community support may occur spontaneously (e.g., the "Review Revolution" on Fanfiction.net [Campbell et al., 2016]), but the creation of affordances by community developers to facilitate this behavior would likely be highly beneficial for beginning writers.

To assist novice writers in actively seeking out mentorship by responding to and encouraging their reviewers, designers of websites that support informal learning communities should work to encourage both the generation and consumption of feedback by increasing the salience of such affordances. Involved adults, such as parents and teachers, should encourage adolescent participation in informal writing communities, or at least avoid discouragement, to allow young writers to engage in these communities and benefit from distributed mentoring. We'll go into more detail on the design implications for learning communities raised by our theory in chapter 6.

In the next section, we turn to the second technique we found useful to scaffold our qualitative research and extend the analysis over our very large data set: an interpretable machine-learning and sentiment-analysis tool developed earlier by Cecilia's research group.

Extending Qualitative Research via Machine Learning and Sentiment Analysis: Beyond Abundance

After our discovery of a clear correlation between lexical diversity and the abundance of distributed mentoring, we wondered if we could find further evidence for the benefits of the other attributes of distributed mentoring. Our thematic analysis of reviews (described in chapter 4) identified a broad variety of review types (thirteen categories), among them targeted positive, targeted corrective or constructive, update encouragement, etc. We speculated that certain review categories might be correlated with various attributes of distributed mentoring. For example, could affect-laden or supportive reviews improve authors' writing? Or were constructive reviews more effective? In order to analyze the full data set in more depth and to delve into the affective or socioemotional component of distributed mentoring, we decided it would be helpful to classify all 177 million reviews in the data set into one of these thirteen categories.

Obviously, however, such a vast undertaking is beyond human capability. Instead, a member of our research group, Jihyun Lee, utilized an existing tool to embark upon this massive project. ALOE (Affect Labeler of Expressions) is a publicly available, open-source machine-learning and sentiment-analysis tool developed by our research group (Brooks et al., 2013) to classify emotion and other characteristics in short, informal text. ALOE utilizes support-vector machines (Cortes & Vapnik, 1995) to train multiple binary classifiers on relatively small, manually coded data sets of short texts, using tenfold cross-validation. It has been shown to be effective on texts with an average length of fifty characters, even shorter than tweets (Brooks et al., 2013). ALOE was developed with the goal of making the extracted feature model as transparent as possible to facilitate qualitative understanding of large text data sets. This is another important tenet of human-centered data science: making sure both the input parameters and the results of automated analyses are easy for humans to comprehend. The reviews left on Fanfiction.net were usually too short to analyze with MTLD, which performs poorly on texts under one hundred words. However, ALOE is perfectly suited to the analysis of such short texts.

Utilizing ALOE, our goal was to systematically categorize the entire review data set into one of the thirteen codes we identified from our qualitative work described in chapter 4, such as shallow positive, targeted positive, targeted constructive, nonconstructive negative, and fandom remarks (see table 4.1 for a detailed list). Given that we already had manually coded 4,499 reviews via the procedure illustrated in chapter 4, we fed these labels to ALOE to extract features for each category. ALOE is a binary classifier and thus works on each category separately. In other words, for a category such as shallow positive, the software examines a review and outputs a binary result stating whether or not it belongs to that category. Because our data fell into thirteen categories rather than only two, for each of our review categories, there were many more negative examples than there were reviews where the code applied (positive examples). This imbalance in labeled data is a common machine-learning problem, and thus many methods exist in the literature for balancing data sets. Empirical tests of ALOE verified that downsampling (randomly removing more-common negative examples) produced the best results in dealing with the imbalance in labeled data (Brooks et al., 2013).

The software takes as input a comma-separated values (CSV) file with the columns "id," "timestamp," "participant," and "message" as defaults. An additional column, "truth," contains ground truth information. Table 5.2 illustrates the feature model and the results of the classifier for each review type.

After conducting tenfold cross-validation to reduce overfitting (detecting patterns in the data that don't generalize beyond the training set), we found that among those thirteen types, only the shallow positive and update encouragement types received precision and recall scores over 0.68. This made sense to us as a manual review of the data demonstrated that some of the other categories contained subtle differences that might be difficult to ascertain. Additionally, ALOE utilizes a "bag of words" approach, where all the ordering information in the source text is discarded, leaving only a list of words that appeared in the review and the number of times each word occurred. Although this approach has been successful for many text-analysis problems (Witten, Frank, & Hall, 2011), overfitting is a real risk, especially for a data set such as ours, which consisted of short reviews that often required contextual knowledge to classify.

To strengthen the results, members of the research team labeled 1,600 additional reviews using the process described in chapter 4 but limited the category labels to shallow positive, targeted positive, targeted constructive, update encouragement, or none of the above. Utilizing this additional training data set, we obtained a total of 6,099 labeled reviews. After several days of processing, ALOE classified 29.8 percent of the reviews in the entire 177-million-review data set as update encouragement, with precision, accuracy, and recall slightly better than in the above table; 46.9 percent as targeted reviews (both positive and constructive), with precision of 79.9 percent, recall of 79.0 percent, and accuracy of 78.0 percent; and 10.2 percent of the 177 million reviews as both update encouragement and targeted. ALOE also classified positive reviews over the entire data set of 177 million reviews (including both shallow positive and targeted positive), with 80.2 percent precision, 84.3 percent recall, and 76.2 percent accuracy.

The successful classification of so much of the full data set enables further qualitative and quantitative analysis. For example, the data could now be studied to determine if one attribute of distributed mentoring may be

Table 5.2
Result of ALOE analysis on thirteen different review types performed on 4,499 manually coded reviews. We conducted tenfold cross-validation to reduce overfitting. Among those thirteen types, the shallow positive and update encouragement types received precision and recall scores over 0.6. (Table by Jihyun Lee.)

Review type	Precision	Recall	Accuracy	Top features
Shallow positive	0.684	0.627	0.768	The, end, plot, stori, her, he, amaz, scene, love, charact
Targeted positive	0.610	0.455	0.749	Made, clever, would, twist, the, end, fabul, duration, mysteri, suppos
Targeted corrective or constructive	0.538	0.315	0.841	Prn_first_sng, throw, grammar, love, negation, appar, attack, altern, thi, french
Targeted positive and corrective/ constructive	0.316	0.103	0.939	Link, reinett, fade, sometim, ahead, voldemort, critic, but, includ, conflict
Nonconstructive negative	0.285	0.044	0.989	Dumbass, holysit …, no …, terribl, toaster, fu***ng, hannah, namist, bore, fuuu …
Discussion about the story	0.401	0.120	0.908	Vote, ventu, heck, altern, regener, sophi, offic, discontinu, agre, oc
Discussion not about the story	0.357	0.058	0.979	Catherin, tate, alonzi, benedict, bi, crazy, harry/shiva, hummer, jip, ps2
Fandom remarks	0.494	0.202	0.898	Canon, accur, imposs, episod, rtd, banish, k, dudlei, season, dramion
One-sided connection	0.355	0.091	0.958	God-k, isol, allow, #;), sadden, bex, almost, flat, ya, heart-wrench
Two-sided connection	0.2	0.035	0.986	Nikki, buddi, argument, ashleyyyi, dedic, mintykay4576, pellinor, safeti, sarash, smo
Review fishing	0.5	0.153	0.997	Bought, fabul, danish, perhap, clip, rosaliehale1997, check, observ, frontdoor6, multi
Update encouragement	0.790	0.716	0.869	Updat, continu, keep, pleas, more, soon, moar, sequel, wait, plz
Miscellaneous	0.375	0.04	0.983	Wat, 100th, 4chan, c2, cruis, dfdsf, eargasm, embarass, flyyyyyyyi, hmmmmm

more effective than others. Perhaps targeted reviews are correlated with greater increases in lexical diversity, as opposed to merely utilizing the number of reviews. This represents ongoing work in our research group.

New Approaches to Distributed Mentoring and Online Communities

This effort raises new questions about distributed mentoring and opens areas for exploration in the study of author-reader interaction in fanfiction communities. By operationalizing the abundance and availability of distributed mentoring as a count of previous reviews, we identified certain attributes of this type of mentoring to be effective on a large scale (Frens et al., 2018). Our work listing other attributes of distributed mentoring (Evans et al., 2017) provides a framework for exploration of review content. Our research group is presently quantitatively examining aggregation, accretion, acceleration, and affect in the 177 million reviews present on Fanfiction.net. Large-scale analysis of review content could expand on this model by demonstrating how the views of different readers synthesize into a greater whole. We hypothesize that given an equal abundance of reviews, a greater diversity of review perspective will be associated with improved outcomes for author learning.

Another potential research area will be to explore roles that users take on within fanfiction communities. We observed in prior work that there is no status or experience distinction among users' profile pages, unlike in most offline settings, unless authors or reviewers choose to report such experience (Campbell et al., 2016). For this reason, the specific affordances of Fanfiction.net provide teens with unique opportunities to assume mentorship roles they may not be able to take on offline. We are conducting a network analysis to analyze roles that may exist in fanfiction communities and how the roles of author and reviewer interact. The modeling and clustering of patterns of role assumption would enable us to further understand distributed mentoring in this community and may lead to implications for design in other learning communities.

The Potential of Distributed Mentoring

In this chapter, we have explained a few of the human-centered data science approaches that can be used to study distributed mentoring in the complex world of fanfiction communities today. We hope these techniques are illustrative of the type of work that needs to be expanded upon in the future as we continue to inhabit a world inundated by human-generated data. Distributed mentoring, in particular, demonstrates the potential of turning this vast and interwoven network of communication to our favor, thus allowing people young and old to learn from one another in ways that are not prescribed or constricted from above—a landscape fostering knowledge, emotion, and identity development. The current age has made it all too clear that there is a potential downside to networked publics and the proliferation of constant connection between all humans of all ages and walks of life. It behooves us to pay attention to novel and unusual methods of learning that extend and multiply from person to person and that are amplified by new technologies in a constructive manner, especially if we want to grow and develop as a society in positive ways. In the final chapter, we move beyond the study of fandom to consider the potentially transformative implications of distributed mentoring across much broader areas of both informal and formal learning.

6 Conclusion: Beyond Fandom

Whenever you tell someone that you're writing a book, they naturally ask what it's about. In our case, the easy thing to say is "It's a book about fanfiction." Having journeyed this far with us, we hope you can appreciate why we're not quite satisfied with giving this answer. Okay, you might say, a more precise characterization would be "It's a book about young people's mentoring experiences in fanfiction communities." This is certainly an improvement and, we suppose, technically accurate. But throughout our research and the writing of this book, we have become convinced that distributed mentoring need not be—indeed, likely is not currently—restricted to a single context. Therefore, we want to use this final chapter to look beyond fandom and consider whether the phenomenon we've described in these pages has broader resonance.

We will consider other online communities that are likely candidates for distributed mentoring, and why. We will also venture to engage in a discussion that some might consider a third rail in education research: what lessons might we draw from our work that could inform the design of formal learning experiences. But before we look beyond fandom, we want to take stock of some key insights we've gained from our research, as well as explore what insights designers of informal learning environments might draw from this work.

Three Insights

The first major insight of our work relates to the nature of the community that arises when people come together around a shared passion and a personal drive to improve their writing and continue the story they love so much. We were struck by the rarity of flaming and trolling in our analysis of story reviews. Words of praise and encouragement far surpassed negative feedback, and story critiques were typically delivered in a respectful way. We are mindful of the likelihood that authors block or delete particularly nasty comments on sites such as Fanfiction.net, and we acknowledge the existence of "toxic fandom" more generally, which manifests in such incidents as *Star Wars* fanboys' online harassment of Kelly Marie Tran, who portrayed the first female main character of color, in 2018. Still, the supportive atmosphere that we observed on the particular sites we selected for our research was hard to dismiss. Our conversations with fanfiction authors affirmed our impressions, as they spoke about the emotional support they consistently received through their participation in fanfiction communities. This positive atmosphere stands in stark contrast to the vitriol found in many other corners of the internet. It also provides a welcome oasis for youth who, like Ruby, have struggled to find community in their everyday lives at home, school, and other offline contexts. For Ruby, the community she discovered through her online fan participation has helped her to define, appreciate, and celebrate aspects of her identity that she previously had trouble expressing to others.

The second insight addresses the transformative role of network-enabled mentoring experiences. Throughout these pages, we have shown how the affordances of networked publics transform mentoring in distinct ways. Affordances such as persistence, asynchronous communication, public and searchable content, and anonymity (or pseudonymity) give rise to a distributed form of mentoring whose power resides in the combined effect of receiving many small pieces of feedback across people, platforms, time, and space. Distributed mentoring depends on the interplay between one tiny unit of feedback and its effect when placed in relationship with other tiny units of feedback left by other people on different days and through diverse channels. This combined effect is captured by the seven attributes of distributed mentoring that we have described in this book: abundance, aggregation, accretion, acceleration, availability, asynchronicity, and affect. We have argued that these attributes describe a new form of mentoring that is more democratic, ad hoc, and tailored to the in-the-moment needs of the writer than traditional forms of mentoring.

The final insight combines the first two by recognizing the learning possibilities that arise when network-enabled mentoring takes place in the context of a positive, supportive community. We heard repeatedly from authors about the growth they experienced as writers through their participation in fanfiction communities. They pointed to the advice shared in writing groups on FIMfiction.net, the reviews they received on their individual stories, and the one-to-one communications through private messaging channels, among other forms and sources of feedback. Our analysis of story reviews showed that a sizable portion of reviews left for authors offer substantive feedback on aspects such as character and plot development. As Ruby noted to us, "If I know which qualities of my writing people like, I can develop my strengths more and incorporate them into future works." And, finally, our longitudinal analysis tracking the lexical diversity of texts—a measure of an author's usage of different words—revealed a positive association with the number of reviews received, even when taking into account the effects of popularity, aging, and practice. Taken together, these findings point to the positive impact of distributed mentoring experiences on authors' development as writers.

Designing for Distributed Mentoring

As researchers interested in the design of learning environments, we have reflected on the design implications of our work. Although we found ample evidence of distributed mentoring on both Fanfiction.net and FIMfiction. net, we also noted the different forms that feedback and participant interaction took on these two platforms. For instance, FIMfiction.net has user groups, whereas Fanfiction.net does not. Several of the authors we interviewed said they rely on the forums in these user groups as resources to improve their writing. The two writing groups we described in chapter 4 illustrate the type of feedback and support that participants typically receive in FIMfiction.net forums and how this feedback aligns with the attributes of distributed mentoring. We found ample evidence for distributed mentoring on Fanfiction.net as well, but it looked slightly different because of the different communication channels available to participants.

Even within FIMfiction.net forums, the way in which these forums shaped communication also mattered. For instance, at the time of our research, forum posts did not have threaded replies. If a member wanted to reply to a comment made by another member, they used double angle brackets (>>) preceded by the name of the person to whom they were addressing their response. This custom meant that members could, in a single post, reference comments from multiple other members. This example shows that the design of specific interaction features matters; these features shape how people engage with one another and, ultimately, the precise forms that distributed mentoring takes. We would therefore encourage designers of online communities to be mindful and deliberate about how they approach the design of participant interaction and communication.

With respect to the design of fanfiction communities in particular, our work inspired us to propose some design considerations that we believe will support distributed mentoring experiences for all authors. Our first suggestion relates to our observation that reviews were unevenly distributed across stories on Fanfiction.net. Some stories had hundreds of reviews, whereas others received only a handful, and some received none at all. In Campbell et al. (2016), we proposed a simple recommender that directs community members who have recently left a review to similar stories that have few or no reviews. Such a system would help draw attention to stories that are in greatest need of feedback. It could also help connect readers and writers to stories that align with their interests, enhancing community engagement.

In the case of authors who regularly receive lots of feedback on their stories, it is sometimes difficult for them to extract the dominant themes and use them to make decisions about how to develop their work. Tools that use text-mining techniques to automatically synthesize common themes or highlight contrasting viewpoints could be one way to enhance the distributed mentoring experiences of popular authors. Whether they receive a large or small number of reviews, most authors value shallow positive feedback. Therefore, providing ways to "like" a story, as is possible on AO3 and some but not all fanfiction repositories, could promote this type of feedback, enhancing the affective dimension of distributed mentoring.

Where in the World (or, at Least, Online) Is Distributed Mentoring?

We have put forward a theory of distributed mentoring based on our extensive research in fanfiction communities. Based on this research, we feel quite confident in asserting (1) the existence of distributed mentoring and (2) its widespread presence in fanfiction communities. But what about other network-enabled affinity spaces? Is distributed mentoring unique to fanfiction communities, or might we expect to find it beyond fandom? We believe that the attributes of distributed mentoring have more to do with the affordances of networked publics in general than they do with fanfiction communities in particular. Let's consider a few online affinity spaces and how they might support distributed mentoring.

DeviantArt is an online community where members display and share their original artwork, photography, and videography. In many ways, DeviantArt feels a lot like a fanfiction community, only with visual art as its focus rather than writing. (In fact, it is possible to find some fanfiction on the site, and one of the site's twenty categories of art is fan art.) Similar to Fanfiction.net and FIMfiction.net, members, or "deviants," maintain profile pages where they share information about themselves and display their creations (called "deviations"). Members leave comments on one another's art, similar to story reviews on fanfiction sites, and they can also communicate through private messaging. There are community forums dedicated to a variety of topics, from politics and philosophy to more site-specific topics such as photography and digital art. In the latter type of forum, members seek and offer advice on various aspects of their craft. In the photography forum, for instance, members ask for technical help using Photoshop, look for suggestions about the best photography gear, and seek advice on taking artistic photographs. In the monthly photography critique threads, members share a photo of their choosing and receive substantive and constructive critiques from other members. One person started a thread to share the series of photography tutorials that he had created, an example of one-to-many mentoring reminiscent of some of the writing groups we observed on FIMfiction.net. At the time of this writing, he had published eighty-five individual tutorials on topics such as how apertures and shutter speeds work, the importance of editing one's photos, and how to take photos at night and in low light.

In view of the similarities in structure and focus between DeviantArt and the fanfiction communities in our study, it's not too difficult to see how distributed mentoring would flourish on DeviantArt. What about online communities that have a totally different focus? What about knitting, for instance? Let's consider the popular online knitting community, Ravelry. Like Fanfiction.net, FIMfiction.net, and DeviantArt, Ravelry functions as an online affinity space that draws together people who share a common passion and desire to improve their skills. Members, or "ravelers," create profiles that include personal information about themselves, such as their location, birthday, years knitting, favorite color, favorite curse word, and a short "about me" description. These profiles form part of a member's personal "notebook," which includes links to finished projects, information about yarn, hook, and needle sizes, and lists of relevant groups, forums, and friends on Ravelry. Members can leave public comments on one another's projects or send private messages directly to others. Forums and groups are places to meet other members, ask craft-specific questions, and receive guidance on tools, equipment, techniques, and patterns. Groups form around location or topic and range from just two members to over thirty thousand members.

What makes Ravelry a good candidate for distributed mentoring? Although knitting represents a different domain than fiction writing or visual art, it is nevertheless a creative pursuit. So does distributed mentoring depend on creative production? Perhaps, if you define creative production in its broadest sense. We would argue that activities as diverse as designing a new skin for *Minecraft*, deriving an elegant solution to an algebra problem, or participating in a citizen science project all represent acts of creation. But acts of creation are not sufficient for distributed mentoring to flourish. These creations must be shared within a community of people who are somehow invested in the particular domain, either as creators, consumers, or both. Without a community of similarly impassioned and knowledgeable people—in other words, without an affinity space—distributed mentoring cannot take hold. It is fueled by this shared passion and knowledge.

Finally, it is no coincidence that the Ravelry interface bears so many similarities to DeviantArt, Fanfiction.net, and FIMfiction.net. In this book, we have described how distributed mentoring depends on the specific affordances of networked publics, particularly their ability to connect people both in groups and through one-to-one channels across time and space. Features such as the ability to send private messages, comment on members' creations, and share ideas in community forums all support the seven attributes of distributed mentoring.

Our brief explorations of DeviantArt and Ravelry underscore three key ingredients for distributed mentoring: (1) a focus on interest-driven creation, (2) the existence of an affinity space, and (3) the support of network-enabled technologies.

And Now, the Third Rail

We approach a discussion about the educational applications of distributed mentoring with some trepidation. After all, is it even possible to take something that is inherently interest driven, open ended, and informal and apply it successfully to a context that has as many external constraints placed on it as our educational system does? We can think of several reasons why it might be a good idea to keep distributed mentoring in the realm of informal affinity spaces. Consider the domain of writing and how it is taught in most public schools in the United States. First, not all students come to school with an existing interest in writing; in fact, many demonstrate a positive aversion. This state of affairs stands in stark contrast to the passion and commitment we witnessed among participants in fanfiction communities, including both Ruby and Cecilia, whose interest in fanfiction was initially sparked by their desire to continue exploring the worlds of their favorite books. Second, there is enormous pressure on teachers, particularly in public schools, to prepare their students to pass state and national standardized tests. This pressure is intensified when high stakes are attached to these tests, such as teacher pay, student graduation requirements, or even the threat of school closure. Third, the Common Core State Standards for English Language Arts lay out comprehensive guidelines about the writing skills that students at various grade levels should be able to demonstrate. Although we believe in the value of the standards enumerated, we note with some regret that the writing-specific standards for high school grades emphasize nonfiction writing. In fact, not one of the fourteen samples of student writing from grades nine through twelve provided in the English Language Arts appendices includes a piece of fiction writing. As a result, a teacher would seem justified to devote as little time as possible to teaching fiction writing. Finally, the structure and pacing of a school day does not seem to lend itself to the type of flexible, open-ended, and organic community we observed in fanfiction communities.

Despite the challenges of working within such a system, we believe that it is an opportune moment to apply the lessons of distributed mentoring to formal educational settings. There is increasing recognition that learning is life long, life wide, and life deep (Banks et al., 2007). Learners of all ages are seeking knowledge outside traditional institutions, for instance, by watching YouTube tutorials, enrolling in massive open online courses

(MOOCs), and participating in Q and A forums. These informal avenues of learning are even starting to translate into real opportunities. Employers are discovering promising job candidates through unlikely channels, such as developers who have earned high reputation scores on Stack Overflow or self-taught data scientists who have won multiple Kaggle Competitions.

Some formal educational institutions are beginning to evolve in response to the emergence of these informal learning opportunities. This shift is most apparent in higher education, where universities are offering a greater variety of online degree programs, and more and more professors are creating MOOCs through Coursera and edX. There are even some notable changes happening at the K–12 level, with innovative models trying to disrupt our current factory-style education system. These models include Quest to Learn (a public 6–12 school designed around game-like quests), Expeditionary Learning Education (a model designed around project-based learning expeditions that emphasizes student engagement, character, and leadership), AltSchool (an educational startup focused on personalized learning experiences), and Global Online Academy (which aims to bring a wide range of flexible, online courses to high school students).

These efforts to disrupt our current education system are driven in part by the recognition that our current system is not serving our youth particularly well. Results from the 2015 Program for International Student Assessment (PISA) show the United States trailing many countries in science, math, and reading scores (Organisation for Economic Cooperation and Development, 2016). The 2011 *Nation's Report Card* on writing showed that only 27 percent of eighth and twelfth graders are scoring at or above the proficient level in writing (US Department of Education, 2012, fig. A). In our own research, we have found evidence for a decline in original, "out of the box" fiction writing among middle and high school students between 1990 and 2011 (Gardner & Davis, 2013; Weinstein, Clark, DiBartolomeo, & Davis, 2014). And, although dropout rates have declined in recent years, there are still over two million youth in the United States designated as high school dropouts (Snyder, de Brey, & Dillow, 2018, table 219.71). Clearly, there is much room for improvement when it comes to educating our young people.

Let's begin with the implications of our work for the way that writing is taught in school. In previous research, we have documented the observations of veteran teachers who have witnessed firsthand the impact on writing instruction of a rising culture of standardized testing (Gardner & Davis, 2013). In such an atmosphere, the five-paragraph essay is the gold standard, and anything that deviates from this standard is not rewarded. What would it look like to subvert this status quo? Let's start by transforming writing instruction from a largely solitary activity to a social, collaborative one.

Our research joins an established body of work pointing to the value of collaborative learning across a variety of subjects (Dillenbourg, 1999; Hmelo-Silver, 2013). Researchers have demonstrated a range of learning benefits that transpire when people come together to work on a shared task (Dillenbourg, 1999; Rogoff, 1998; Roschelle & Teasley, 1995; Selman, 1975). Learners build off one another to generate ideas, they push one another to think in new ways, and, in ideal circumstances, they produce solutions that are more complex and interesting than any person could have produced individually. Further, learning is highly engaging when it is grounded in authentic interactions with peers and friends (Ito et al., 2013).

With the widespread adoption of networked technologies, people can now collaborate without having to come together physically (Stahl et al., 2006). This flexible connectivity means that learners from diverse geographic and cultural backgrounds are able to participate in shared learning experiences (Ito et al., 2013). Scholars in the field of computer-supported collaborative learning (CSCL) have shown how the affordances of networked technologies can support meaningful collaborative learning experiences, particularly when CSCL environments incorporate a social functionality (e.g., Kreijns & Kirschner, 2004; Kirschner, Strijbos, Kreijns, & Beers, 2004).

With this body of research in mind, we believe that open, community-based systems that connect students across school districts, states, or even countries could be used successfully to foster the multiple sources of feedback that authors said they value in online fanfiction communities. We deliberately use *systems* in its plural form to emphasize that we do not imagine a one-size-fits-all approach to building online communities that support distributed mentoring in formal education contexts. At the same time, we do imagine that such platforms would share some common features. Based on the insights from our research, such systems would work best if students could present themselves pseudonymously to help stave off inhibitions associated with giving and receiving feedback.

To that end, we recommend that students interact with other students outside of their own school (asynchronicity). Looking beyond the four walls of the classroom or school would also make it possible to form large communities of learners, thus increasing the amount of feedback that any one student receives and the speed with which they receive it (acceleration, abundance). In addition to serving a motivational function for students, engaging in large, open communities would also expose students to diverse perspectives that inspire them to expand their thinking. Recognizing the importance of bringing fanfiction authors and readers together around a shared passion for a particular fandom, we suggest making every effort to connect students who share an existing interest that could be used as a focus in their writing (affect). Teachers could serve as coaches for their students by helping them to provide constructive feedback and build on feedback provided by other students (accretion), as well as helping students to learn from and make use of the disparate feedback they receive (aggregation, availability). Teachers could even serve as community moderators, ensuring that discourse among community members remains civil and supportive (affect). And lastly, although writing is the most obvious test case to explore in light of our research, it need not be the only domain of learning supported by distributed mentoring.

Of course, we are not the first ones to propose connecting students across geographic and temporal boundaries to create unique and meaningful learning experiences. Take, for instance, Out of Eden Learn, an online program that brings together students of similar ages across geographic settings to engage in shared learning experiences. The program was developed by researchers at Harvard Project Zero in conjunction with the twenty-one-thousand-mile walk begun in 2013 by journalist and National Geographic fellow Paul Salopek, which follows the ancient pathways of human migration (his walk continues at the time of this book's publication in 2019). Using a custom-built social media platform, Out of Eden Learn engages students in eight-to twelve-week learning experiences in which they are encouraged to: "(1) slow down to observe the world carefully and listen attentively to others; (2) exchange stories and perspectives with one another; and (3) make connections between their own lives and bigger human stories." To date, the program has served over twenty thousand students in fifty-seven countries (Out of Eden Learn, n.d.).

We believe that interactive online programs such as Out of Eden Learn represent promising ways to support distributed mentoring in formal educational settings. Such programs connect a wide range of students across space and time, and they provide the scaffolding needed to engage students in meaningful conversations about their lived experiences. Through these distributed conversations, students learn about cultures and perspectives different from their own, which, ideally, will encourage them to expand their thinking in new ways.

Outside the Secret Garden

The September 2017 issue of the *Atlantic* featured an article titled "Have Smartphones Destroyed a Generation?" Written by Jean Twenge, a professor at San Diego State University, and based on her book *iGen: Why Today's Super-Connected Kids Are Growing Up Less Rebellious, More Tolerant, Less Happy—and Completely Unprepared for Adulthood—and What That Means for the Rest of Us* (Twenge, 2017), the article explores whether smartphones and social media are responsible for a host of disturbing trends among young people over recent decades, such as increased rates of suicide, depression, and loneliness. As one might expect from the titles of both the article and the book, Twenge's answer is yes. Rather than delve into the specifics of the evidence that Twenge marshals to come to this conclusion (Katie has done that elsewhere, see Davis, Weinstein, & Gardner, 2017), we want simply to offer this book as a counternarrative to this pessimistic—and, it seems, dominant—view of youth and networked technologies.

Of course, Twenge did not focus on fanfiction communities in her research, just as most youth do not participate in these communities. But we believe that paying attention to what is going on in this "secret garden" is worthwhile—indeed, necessary. It can show us how networked technologies, when they are put to good use, succeed in supporting young people in their quest for identity, community, and rich learning experiences. In this book, we have focused primarily on the latter by describing the distinct characteristics of distributed mentoring and showing how this new form of network-enabled mentoring can support youth in their development as writers. But we trust that the quotes from our interview participants, as well as the personal stories of Ruby and Cecilia, have made it clear that these mentoring experiences exist within a much broader context of participation, community, and personal growth. Therefore, just as we believe that the benefits of distributed mentoring can be experienced in other contexts—including formal education settings—so too are we optimistic that the broader context of fanfiction communities can be experienced more widely by young people, fans and nonfans alike. We have no illusions that it is a simple matter to export the magic of the secret garden. We hope that the insights from our work provide a starting point.

Appendix: Fanfiction Database Schema

The tables below document our database schema. There are seventeen tables in total. Table 1 contains metadata information, and tables 2 through 17 list all columns in each table in our database and how those database tables are related to one another. All date-related columns are written in Coordinated Universal Time (UTC) format to avoid time zone issues. (Data collected by Jihyun Lee.)

Table 1

Metainformation of the sixteen tables stored in the database "fanfictiondrg201701"

Name	Relevance	# Rows	# Columns	Size (MB)
category	story	9	2	0.05
character	story	49,651	2	6.55
fandom	story	10,423	4	3.69
genre	story	20	2	0.05
language	story	44	2	0.05
location	user	249	2	0.03
rating	story	4	2	0.05
review	review	176,715,206	6	56,947.00
story	story	6,828,943	15	1,275.52
story_character	story	10,052,628	2	612.38
story_content	story	28,493,311	4	546,974.94
story_genre	story	10,525,966	2	573.25
user	user	8,492,507	3	857.30
user_favorite_author	user	32,566,785	2	2,379.98
user_favorite_story	user	160,217,066	2	11,236.00
user_profile	user	8,492,507	7	7,092.72

Table 2

Table "category"

Column name	Type	Description	Range
id	Int(11)	ID given to each category in the database	1–9
name	varchar(128)	Name of the category	{anime, book, cartoon, comic, game, misc, movie, play, tv}

Table 3

Table "character"

Column name	Type	Description	Range
id	Int(11)	ID given to each character in the database	1–49,651
name	varchar(128)	Name of the character	{Emma C., Julian B., Kieran ...}

Table 4

Table "fandom"

Column name	Type	Description	Range
id	Int(11)	ID given to each fandom in the database	1–10,423
category_id	Int(11)	Database ID of category. This can be joined with `category`.`id`.	1–9
name	varchar(128)	Name of the fandom	{Naruto, Hetalia—xis Powers, Inuyasha ...}
url	varchar(2000)	URL text of the fandom. Appending this URL text to "[sitename]" will give you the link.	{/anime/Naruto/, /anime/Hetalia—Axis Powers/, /anime/Inuyasha/...}

Table 5

Table "genre"

Column name	Type	Description	Range
id	Int(11)	ID given to each category type in the database	1–21
name	varchar(128)	Name of the genre	{Romance, Drama, Hurt/Comfort ...}

Table 6

Table "language"

Column name	Type	Description	Range
id	Int(11)	ID given to each category type in the database	1–44
name	varchar(128)	Name of the language. This is joined with the story and says in which language the story was written.	{English, Spanish, Italian ...}

Table 7

Table "location"

Column name	Type	Description	Range
id	int(11)	ID given to each category type in the database	1–249
name	varchar(128)	Name of the location (i.e., country)	{Korea, Democratic, USA, UK ...}

Table 8

Table "rating"

Column name	Type	Description	Range
id	int(11)	ID given to each category type in the database	1–4
name	varchar(45)	Name of the rating. K is "Intended for general audience 5 years and older. Content should be free of any coarse language, violence, and adult themes." K+ is "Suitable for more mature children, 9 years and older, with minor action violence without serious injury. May contain mild coarse language. Should not contain any adult themes." T is "Suitable for teens, 13 years and older, with some violence, minor coarse language, and minor suggestive adult themes." M is "Not suitable for children or teens below the age of 16 with non-explicit suggestive adult themes, references to some violence, or coarse language."	{K, K+, T, M}

Table 9

Table "review"

Column name	Type	Description	Range
id	int(11)	ID given to each category type in the database	1–176,715,206
user_id	int(11)	Database ID of user. This can be joined with `user`.`id`.	1–8,492,509
story_id	int(11)	Database ID of story. This can be joined with `story`.`id`.	1–6,828,943
date	int(10)	Date the review was written	0–1,486,831,827
chapter	int(11)	The chapter of the story for which the review was written	0–65,535
content	mediumtext	Content of the review	...

Table 10

Table "story"

Column name	Type	Description	Range
id	int(11)	ID given to each category type in the database. This can be joined with any columns named `story_id`.	1–6,828,943
fandom_id	int(11)	Database ID of fandom. This can be joined with `fandom`.`id`.	1–10,423
user_id	int(11)	Database ID of user. This can be joined with `user`.`id`.	1–1,520,309
rating_id	int(11)	Database ID of rating. This can be joined with `rating`.`id`.	1–4
language_id	int(11)	Database ID of language. This can be joined with `language`.`id`.	1–44
ff_story_id	int(11)	Fanfiction ID given from the fanfiction website. You can access the story page on [sitename] through the link "[sitename]/s/<ff_story_id>."	4–12,240,198
title	varchar(256)	Title of the story	...
chapters	int(11)	Number of chapters of this story written so far	1–2,182
words	int(11)	Number of words written for this story	0–12,751,087
reviews	int(11)	Number of reviews written for this story. (This includes the reviews written for deleted chapters.)	0–46,058
favorites	int(11)	Number of favorites received	0–20,597
followers	int(11)	Number of followers	0–20,275
date_published	int(10)	Date this story was published for the first time	0–1,479,619,531
date_updated	int(10)	Date this story was updated.	-1–1,479,619,960
is_complete	tinyint(1)	A number that indicates whether this story is complete or not. 0 means the story is not complete; 1 means the story is.	{0, 1}

Table 11

Table "story_character"

Column name	Type	Description	Range
story_id	Int(11)	Database ID of story. This can be joined with `story`.`id`.	1–6,828,900
character_id	Int(11)	Database ID of character. This can be joined with `character`.`id`.	1–49,651

Table 12

Table "story_content"

Column name	Type	Description	Range
story_id	int(11)	Database ID of story. This can be joined with `story`.`id`. You can access the story chapter page on [sitename] through the link "[sitename]/s/<ff_story_id>/<chapter>."	1–6,828,943
chapter	int(11)	Chapter number	0–2,182
chapter_title	varchar(256)	Title of the chapter	...
content	mediumtext	Content of this chapter	...

Table 13

Table "story_genre"

Column name	Type	Description	Range
story_id	Int(11)	Database ID of story. This can be joined with `story`.`id`.	1–6,828,943
genre_id	Int(11)	Database ID of genre. This can be joined with `genre`.`id`.	1–21

Table 14

Table "user"

Column name	Type	Description	Range
id	int(11)	ID given to each category type in the database	1–8,492,509
ff_id	int(11)	Fanfiction user ID given from the fanfiction website. This can be joined with any columns named `user_id`. You can access the user profile page on [sitename] through the link "[sitename]/u/<ff_id>."	3,236–8,780,620
name	varchar(512)	Name of the user	{Fangirl Shipper, Inferno, Vern …}

Table 15

Table "user_favorite_author"

Column name	Type	Description	Range
user_id	int(11)	Database ID of user. This can be joined with `user`.`id`.	1–8,492,310
favorite_user_id	int(11)	Database ID of user favorited by `user_id`. This can be joined with `user`.`id`.	1–8,482,308

Table 16

Table "user_favorite_story"

Column name	Type	Description	Range
user_id	int(11)	Database ID of user. This can be joined with `user`.`id`.	1–8,492,314
story_id	int(11)	Database ID of story. This can be joined with `story`.`id`.	1–6,828,941

Table 17

Table "user_profile"

Column name	Type	Description	Range
user_id	int(11)	Database ID of user. This can be joined with `user`.`id`.	1–8,492,319
location_id	int(11)	Database ID of location. This can be joined with `location`.`id`.	1–249
join_date	int(10)	Date the user joined fanfiction community	-1–1,480,715,936
update_date	int(10)	Date the user updated his/ her profile	-1–1,481,004,293
bio	mediumtext	Biography content written by the user	…
age	tinyint	Self-reported age extracted from the bio content	10–99
gender	char(6)	Self-reported gender extracted from the bio content	{male, female, other}

References

Alexa (2017). Fanfiction.net traffic statistics. Retrieved April 25, 2017, from https://www.alexa.com/siteinfo/fanfiction.net

Altintaş, A. K. (2013). A new Hermione: Re-creations of the female *Harry Potter* protagonist in fan fiction. *Zeitschrift für Anglistik und Amerikanistik: A Quarterly of Language, Literature and Culture, 61,* 155–173. doi:10.1515/zaa.2013.61.2.155

Aragon, C., Hutto, C., Echenique, A., Fiore-Gartland, B., Huang, Y., Kim, J., ... Bayer, J. (2016). Developing a research agenda for human-centered data science. In D. Gergle, M. R. Morris, P. Bjørn, & J. Konstan (Chairs), *Proceedings of the 19th ACM Conference on Computer-Supported Cooperative Work and Social Computing Companion* (pp. 529–535). doi:10.1145/2818052.2855518

Aragon, C. R., Poon, S. S., Monroy-Hernández, A., & Aragon, D. (2009). A tale of two online communities: Fostering collaboration and creativity in scientists and children. In N. Bryan-Kinns, M. D. Gross, H. Johnson, J. Ox, & R. Wakkary (Chairs), *Proceedings of the Seventh ACM Conference on Creativity and Cognition* (pp. 9–18). doi:10.1145/1640233.1640239

Aragon, C. R., & Williams, A. (2011). Collaborative creativity: A complex systems model with distributed affect. In D. Tan, G. Fitzpatrick, C. Gutwin, B. Begole, & W. A. Kellogg (Chairs), *Proceedings of the SIGCHI Conference on Human Factors in Computing Systems* (pp. 1875–1884). doi:10.1145/1978942.1979214

Archive of Our Own. (n.d.). Retrieved May 1, 2018, from https://archiveofourown.org/

Austin, A. E. (2002). Preparing the next generation of faculty: Graduate school as socialization to the academic career. *Journal of Higher Education, 73,* 94–122. doi:10.1080/00221546.2002.11777132

Bacon-Smith, C. (1992). *Enterprising women: Television fandom and the creation of popular myth.* Philadelphia: University of Pennsylvania Press.

Baker-Whitelaw, G. (2014, August 25). How the growing generation gap is changing the face of fandom. *Daily Dot*. Retrieved from https://www.dailydot.com/via/growing-generation-gap-changing-face-fandom/

Baker-Whitelaw, G. (2015, February 23). What not to do when teaching a class about fanfiction. *Daily Dot*. Retrieved from https://www.dailydot.com/irl/berkeley-fanfiction-class-backlash/

Baker-Whitelaw, G., & Romano, A. (2014, June 17). A guide to fanfiction for people who can't stop getting it wrong. *Daily Dot*. Retrieved from https://www.dailydot.com/parsec/complete-guide-to-fanfiction/

Banks, J. A., Au, K. H., Ball, A. F., Bell, P., Gordon, E. W., Gutiérrez, K. D., ... Zhou, M. (2007). *Learning in and out of school in diverse environments: Life-long, life-wide, life-deep*. Retrieved from LIFE Center (Learning in Informal and Formal Environments Center) website: http://life-slc.org/docs/Banks_etal-LIFE-Diversity-Report.pdf

Barenblat, R. (2014). Fan fiction and midrash: Making meaning. *Transformative Works and Cultures, 17*. doi:10.3983/twc.2014.0596

Barron, B., Martin, C. K., Takeuchi, L., & Fithian, R. (2009). Parents as learning partners in the development of technological fluency. *International Journal of Learning and Media, 1*(2), 55–77. doi:10.1162/ijlm.2009.0021

Bates, E., & Goodman, J. C. (1999). On the emergence of grammar from the lexicon. In B. MacWhinney (Ed.), *The emergence of language* (pp. 29–79). Retrieved from https://www.taylorfrancis.com/books/e/9781135676926/chapters/10.4324%2F9781410602367-7

Bauerlein, M. (2008). *The dumbest generation: How the digital age stupefies young Americans and jeopardizes our future (or, don't trust anyone under 30)*. New York, NY: Jeremy P. Tarcher/Penguin.

Beam, M., Chen, C., & Greenberger, E. (2002). The nature of adolescents' relationships with their "very important" nonparental adults. *American Journal of Community Psychology, 30*, 305–325. doi:10.1023/A:1014641213440

Bell, A. (2015, September 1). A brief history of fan fiction. *How We Get to Next*. Retrieved from https://howwegettonext.com/a-brief-history-of-fan-fiction-81c3a54ff5ad

Black, R. W. (2006). Language, culture, and identity in online fanfiction. *E-Learning, 3*, 170–184. doi:10.2304/elea.2006.3.2.170

Black, R. W. (2007). Digital design: English language learners and reader reviews in online fiction. In M. Knobel & C. Lankshear (Eds.), *A new literacies sampler* (pp. 115–136). New York, NY: Peter Lang.

Black, R. W. (2008). *Adolescents and online fan fiction*. New York, NY: Peter Lang.

Blackwell, J. E. (1989). Mentoring: An action strategy for increasing minority faculty. *Academe, 75*(5), 8–14. doi:10.2307/40249734

Boellstorff, T., Nardi, B., Pearce, C., & Taylor, T. L. (2012). *Ethnography and virtual worlds: A handbook of method*. Princeton, NJ: Princeton University Press.

boyd, d. (2007a). The role of networked publics in teenage social life. In D. Buckingham (Ed.), *Youth, identity, and digital media* (pp. 119–142). Cambridge, MA: MIT Press.

boyd, d. (2007b). Why youth (heart) social network sites: The role of networked publics in teenage social life. In D. Buckingham (Ed.), *Youth, identity, and digital media* (pp. 119–142). Cambridge, MA: MIT Press.

Bozeman, B., & Feeney, M. K. (2007). Toward a useful theory of mentoring: A conceptual analysis and critique. *Administration & Society, 39*, 719–739. doi:10.1177/0095399707304119

Bradshaw, T. (2004). *Reading at risk: A survey of literary reading in America* (Research Division Report No. 46). Retrieved from National Endowment for the Arts website: https://www.arts.gov/sites/default/files/ReadingAtRisk.pdf

Brooks, M., Kuksenok, K., Torkildson, M. K., Perry, D., Robinson, J. J., Scott, T. J., … Aragon, C. R. (2013). Statistical affect detection in collaborative chat. In A. Bruckman, S. Counts, C. Lampe, & L. Terveen (Chairs), *Proceedings of the 2013 Conference on Computer Supported Cooperative Work* (pp. 317–328). doi:10.1145/2441776.2441813

Brown, M. C., II, Davis, G. L., & McClendon, S. A. (2000). Mentoring graduate students of color: Myths, models, and modes. *Peabody Journal of Education, 74*(2), 105–118. doi:10.1207/s15327930pje7402_9

Bury, R. (2005). *Cyberspaces of their own: Female fandoms online*. New York, NY: Peter Lang.

Busse, K. (2015). Fan labor and feminism: Capitalizing on the fannish labor of love. *Cinema Journal, 54*(3), 110–115. doi:10.1353/cj.2015.0034

Busse, K. (2017). *Framing fan fiction: Literary and social practices in fan fiction communities*. Iowa City, IA: University of Iowa Press.

Busse, K., & Hellekson, K. (2006). Introduction: Work in progress. In K. Hellekson & K. Busse (Eds.), *Fan fiction and fan communities in the age of the internet: New essays* (pp. 5–32). Jefferson, NC: McFarland.

Busse, K., & Hellekson, K. (2012). Identity, ethics, and fan privacy. In K. Larsen & L. S. Zubernis (Eds.), *Fan culture: Theory/practice* (pp. 38–56). Newcastle-upon-Tyne, England: Cambridge Scholars.

Campbell, J., Aragon, C., Davis, K., Evans, S., Evans, A., & Randall, D. (2016). Thousands of positive reviews: Distributed mentoring in online fan communities. In D. Gergle, M. R. Morris, P. Bjørn, & J. Konstan (Chairs), *Proceedings of the 19th ACM Conference on Computer-Supported Cooperative Work & Social Computing* (pp. 691–704). doi:10.1145/2818048.2819934

Chandler-Olcott, K., & Mahar, D. (2003). Adolescents' anime-inspired "fanfictions": An exploration of multiliteracies. *Journal of Adolescent & Adult Literacy, 46,* 556–566. Retrieved from https://www.jstor.org/stable/40015457

Charmaz, K. (2006). *Constructing grounded theory: A practical guide through qualitative analysis.* London, England: Sage.

Chatelain, M. (2012). *Harry Potter* and the prisoner of copyright law: Fan fiction, derivative works, and the fair use doctrine. *Tulane Journal of Technology and Intellectual Property, 15,* 199–217.

Chen, M. (2012). *Leet noobs: The life and death of an expert player group in* World of Warcraft. New York, NY: Peter Lang.

Coker, C. (2008). The friends of Darkover: An annotated bibliography and history. *Foundation: The International Review of Science Fiction, 37*(104), 42–66.

Coleman, E. G. (2012). *Coding freedom: The ethics and aesthetics of hacking.* Princeton, NJ: Princeton University Press.

Computing Research Association. (1995). CRA-W Distributed Mentor Project. Retrieved February 2, 2019, from ftp://ftp.cs.wisc.edu/cra-mentor/CRA_desc.html

Coppa, F. (2006). A brief history of media fandom. In K. Hellekson & K. Busse (Eds.), *Fan fiction and fan communities in the age of the internet* (pp. 41–59). Jefferson, NC: McFarland.

Cortes, C., & Vapnik, V. (1995). Support-vector networks. *Machine Learning, 20,* 273–297. doi:10.1023/A:1022627411411

Covington, M. A., & McFall, J. D. (2010). Cutting the Gordian knot: The moving-average type–token ratio (MATTR). *Journal of Quantitative Linguistics, 17,* 94–100. doi:10.1080/09296171003643098

Crisp, G., & Cruz, I. (2009). Mentoring college students: A critical review of the literature between 1990 and 2007. *Research in Higher Education, 50,* 525–545. doi:10.1007/s11162-009-9130-2

Crossley, S. A., Salsbury, T., McNamara, D. S., & Jarvis, S. (2011). Predicting lexical proficiency in language learner texts using computational indices. *Language Testing, 28,* 561–580. doi:10.1177/0265532210378031

Curtis, P. (1997). Mudding: Social phenomena in text-based virtual realities. In S. Kiesler (Ed.), *Culture of the internet* (pp. 121–142). Mahwah, NJ: Lawrence Erlbaum.

Davis, K. (2010). Coming of age online: The developmental underpinnings of girls' blogs. *Journal of Adolescent Research, 25*, 145–171. doi:10.1177/0743558409350503

Davis, K., & Weinstein, E. (2017). Identity development in the digital age: An Eriksonian perspective. In M. F. Wright (Ed.), *Identity, sexuality, and relationships among emerging adults in the digital age* (pp. 1–17). Hershey, PA: Information Science Reference.

Davis, K., Weinstein, E., & Gardner, H. (2017, August 13). In defense of complexity: Beware of simplistic narratives about teens and technology [Blog post]. Retrieved from https://medium.com/@kedavis/in-defense-of-complexity-beware-of-simplistic -narratives-about-teens-and-technology-f9a7cb59176

Dawson, P. (2014). Beyond a definition: Toward a framework for designing and specifying mentoring models. *Educational Researcher, 43*, 137–145. doi:10.3102/ 0013189X14528751

De Kosnik, A. (2016). *Rogue archives: Digital cultural memory and media fandom* [IEEE Xplore Digital Library version]. Retrieved from https://ieeexplore.ieee.org/servlet/ opac?bknumber=7845160

De Kosnik, A., El Ghaoui, L., Cuntz-Leng, V., Godbehere, A., Horbinski, A., Hutz, A., … Pham, V. (2015). Watching, creating, and archiving: Observations on the quantity and temporality of fannish productivity in online fan fiction archives. *Convergence: The International Journal of Research into New Media Technologies, 21*, 145–164. doi:10.1177/1354856514560313

Dillenbourg, P. (1999). What do you mean by collaborative learning? In P. Dillenbourg (Ed.), *Collaborative learning: Cognitive and computational approaches* (pp. 1–19). Oxford, England: Pergamon.

Dinsman, M. (2016). The digital in the humanities: A special interview series. *Los Angeles Review of Books*. Retrieved from https://lareviewofbooks.org/feature/the -digital-in-the-humanities

Domo. (2017). Data never sleeps 5.0 [Infographic]. Retrieved from https://www .domo.com/learn/data-never-sleeps-5

DUB. (n.d.). Retrieved May 1, 2018, from http://dub.uw.edu/

DuBois, D. L., & Silverthorn, N. (2005). Natural mentoring relationships and adolescent health: Evidence from a national study. *American Journal of Public Health, 95*, 518–524. doi:10.2105/AJPH.2003.031476

Durán, P., Malvern, D., Richards, B., & Chipere, N. (2004). Developmental trends in lexical diversity. *Applied Linguistics, 25*, 220–242. doi:10.1093/applin/25.2.220

Dwork, C. (2008). Differential privacy: A survey of results. In M. Agrawal, D. Du, Z. Duan, & A. Li (Eds.), *Lecture Notes in Computer Science: Vol. 4978. Theory and Application of Models of Computation* (pp. 1–19). doi:10.1007/978-3-540-79228-4-1

Dwork, C. (2011). A firm foundation for private data analysis. *Communications of the ACM, 54*(1), 86–95. doi:10.1145/1866739.1866758

Dym, B., & Fiesler, C. (2018). Vulnerable and online: Fandom's case for stronger privacy norms and tools. In V. Evers, M. Naaman, G. Fitzpatrick, K. Karahalios, A. Lampinen, A. Monroy-Hernández (Eds.), *Companion of the 2018 ACM Conference on Computer-Supported Cooperative Work and Social Computing* (pp. 329–332). doi:10.1145/3272973.3274089

Eby, L. T., Rhodes, J. E., & Allen, T. D. (2010). Definition and evolution of mentoring. In T. D. Allen & L. T. Eby (Eds.), *The Blackwell handbook of mentoring: A multiple perspectives approach* (pp. 7–20). Malden, MA: Blackwell.

Ensher, E. A., Heun, C., & Blanchard, A. (2003). Online mentoring and computer-mediated communication: New directions in research. *Journal of Vocational Behavior, 63*, 264–288. doi:10.1016/S0001-8791(03)00044-7

Erickson, L. D., McDonald, S., & Elder, G. H., Jr. (2009). Informal mentors and education: Complementary or compensatory resources? *Sociology of Education, 82*, 344–367. doi:10.1177/003804070908200403

Evans, S., Davis, K., Evans, A., Campbell, J. A., Randall, D. P., Yin, K., & Aragon, C. (2017). More than peer production: Fanfiction communities as sites of distributed mentoring. In C. P. Lee, S. Poltrock, L. Barkhuus, M. Borges, & W. Kellogg (Chairs), *Proceedings of the 2017 ACM Conference on Computer Supported Cooperative Work and Social Computing* (pp. 259–272). doi:10.1145/2998181.2998342

Fanfiction. (n.d.). In Fanlore. Retrieved November 14, 2017, from https://fanlore.org/wiki/Fanfiction

Fergadiotis, G., Wright, H. H., & Green, S. B. (2015). Psychometric evaluation of lexical diversity indices: Assessing length effects. *Journal of Speech, Language, and Hearing Research, 58*, 840–852. doi:10.1044/2015_JSLHR-L-14-0280

Fiesler, C. (2008). Everything I need to know I learned from fandom: How existing social norms can help shape the next generation of user-generated content. *Vanderbilt Journal of Entertainment and Technology Law, 10*, 729–762. Retrieved from http://www.jetlaw.org/wp-content/journal-pdfs/Fiesler.pdf

Fiesler, C., & Bruckman, A. S. (2014). Remixers' understandings of fair use online. In S. Fussell, W. Lutters, M. R. Morris, & M. Reddy (Chairs), *Proceedings of the 17th ACM Conference on Computer Supported Cooperative Work & Social Computing* (pp. 1023–1032). doi:10.1145/2531602.2531695

Fiesler, C., Feuston, J. L., & Bruckman, A. S. (2015). Understanding copyright law in online creative communities. In D. Cosley, A. Forte, L. Ciolfi, & D. McDonald (Chairs), *Proceedings of the 18th ACM Conference on Computer Supported Cooperative Work & Social Computing* (pp. 116–129). doi:10.1145/2675133.2675234

Fiesler, C., Lampe, C., & Bruckman, A. (2016). Reality and perception of copyright terms of service for online content creation. In D. Gergle, M. R. Morris, P. Bjørn, & J. Konstan (Chairs), *Proceedings of the 19th ACM Conference on Computer-Supported Cooperative Work & Social Computing* (pp. 1450–1461). doi:10.1145/2818048.2819931

Fiesler, C., Morrison, S., & Bruckman, A. S. (2016). An archive of their own: A case study of feminist HCI and values in design. In J. Kaye, A. Druin, C. Lampe, D. Morris, & J. P. Hourcade (Chairs), *Proceedings of the 2016 CHI Conference on Human Factors in Computing Systems* (pp. 2574–2585). doi:10.1145/2858036.2858409

FIMfiction.net. (2019). Statistics. Retrieved February 2, 2019, from http://www.fimfiction.net/statistics

Fleiss, J. L., Levin, B., & Paik, M. C. (2003). *Statistical methods for rates and proportions* (3rd ed.) [Wiley Online Library version]. doi:10.1002/0471445428

Flores, A. (2015). Empowerment and civic surrogacy: Community workers' perceptions of their own and their Latino/a students' civic potential. *Anthropology & Education Quarterly, 46*, 397–413. doi:10.1111/aeq.12118

Frens, J., Davis, R., Lee, J., Zhang, D., & Aragon, C. (2018, August). *Reviews matter: How distributed mentoring predicts lexical diversity on fanfiction.net.* Paper presented at the Connected Learning Summit, Cambridge, MA.

Gardner, H., & Davis, K. (2013). *The app generation: How today's youth navigate identity, intimacy, and imagination in a digital world.* New Haven, CT: Yale University Press.

Gee, J. P. (2004). *Situated language and learning: A critique of traditional schooling.* New York, NY: Routledge.

Gee, J. P. (2013). *The anti-education era: Creating smarter students through digital learning.* New York, NY: Palgrave Macmillan.

Geertz, C. (1973). Thick description: Toward an interpretive theory of culture. In *The interpretation of cultures* (pp. 3–32). New York, NY: Basic Books.

Glaser, B. G., & Strauss, A. L. (1967). *The discovery of grounded theory: Strategies for qualitative research.* Chicago, IL: Aldine.

Goffman, E. (1959). *The presentation of self in everyday life.* New York, NY: Anchor Books.

Guerrero-Pico, M., Establés, M.-J., & Ventura, R. (2018). Killing off Lexa: 'Dead Lesbian Syndrome' and intra-fandom management of toxic fan practices in an online queer community. *Participations: Journal of Audience and Reception Studies, 15*(1), 311–333. Retrieved from http://www.participations.org/Volume%2015/Issue%201/17 .pdf

Hafeez, K. (2015, February 23). Two dogs speak as their owner uses the computer [Cartoon]. *The New Yorker.* Retrieved from https://condenaststore.com/featured/two-dogs-speak-as-their-owner-uses-the-computer-kaamran-hafeez.html

Haggard, D. L., Dougherty, T. W., Turban, D. B., & Wilbanks, J. E. (2011). Who is a mentor? A review of evolving definitions and implications for research. *Journal of Management, 37,* 280–304. doi:10.1177/0149206310386227

Halbert, D. (2006). Feminist interpretations of intellectual property. *American University Journal of Gender, Social Policy, and the Law, 14,* 431–460. Retrieved from https:// digitalcommons.wcl.american.edu/jgspl/vol14/iss3/1/

Hall, J. C. (2003). *Mentoring and young people: A literature review.* Retrieved from ERIC database. (ED475263)

Hampton, D. R. (2015). Bound princes and monogamy warnings: *Harry Potter,* slash, and queer performance in LiveJournal communities. *Transformative Works and Cultures, 18.* doi:10.3983/twc.2015.0609

Heath, S. B., & Street, B. V. (2008). *On ethnography: Approaches to language and literacy research.* New York, NY: Teachers College Press.

Hellekson, K., & Busse, K. (Eds.). (2006). *Fan fiction and fan communities in the age of the Internet: New essays.* Jefferson, NC: McFarland.

Hellekson, K., & Busse, K. (2014). *The fan fiction studies reader.* Iowa City, IA: University of Iowa Press.

Higgins, M. C., & Kram, K. E. (2001). Reconceptualizing mentoring at work: A developmental network perspective. *Academy of Management Review, 26,* 264–288. doi:10.5465/AMR.2001.4378023

Hill, M. (2016, July 3). The forgotten early history of fanfiction. *Motherboard.* Retrieved from https://motherboard.vice.com/en_us/article/4xa4wq/the-forgotten -early-history-of-fanfiction

Hills, M. (2002). *Fan cultures.* London, England: Routledge.

Hinck, A. (2012). Theorizing a public engagement keystone: Seeing fandom's integral connection to civic engagement through the case of the *Harry Potter* Alliance. *Transformative Works and Cultures, 10.* doi:10.3983/twc.2012.0311

Hmelo-Silver, C. E. (Ed.) (2013). *The international handbook of collaborative learning*. New York, NY: Routledge.

Hollan, J., Hutchins, E., & Kirsh, D. (2000). Distributed cognition: Toward a new foundation for human–computer interaction research. *ACM Transactions on Computer-Human Interaction (TOCHI)*, *7*, 174–196. doi:10.1145/353485.353487

Human-Centered Data Science Lab. (n.d.). Distributed mentoring in fanfiction communities. Retrieved January 24, 2019, from https://depts.washington.edu/hdsl/research/distributed-mentoring/

Humberd, B., & Rouse, E. (2016). Seeing you in me and me in you: Personal identification in the phases of mentoring relationships. *The Academy of Management Review*, *41*, 435–455. doi:10.5465/amr.2013.0203

Hunt, D., & Michael, C. (1983). Mentorship: A career training and development tool. *The Academy of Management Review*, *8*, 475–485. doi:10.5465/amr.1983.4284603

Hurtado, S., Engberg, M. E., Ponjuan, L., & Landreman, L. (2002). Students' precollege preparation for participation in a diverse democracy. *Research in Higher Education*, *43*, 163–186. doi:10.1023/A:1014467607253

Hutchins, E. (1995). *Cognition in the wild*. Cambridge, MA: MIT Press.

Hutchins, E., & Klausen, T. (1996). Distributed cognition in an airline cockpit. In Y. Engeström & D. Middleton (Eds.), *Cognition and communication at work* (pp. 15–34). Cambridge, England: Cambridge University Press.

Irby, B. J., & Boswell, J. (2016). Historical print context of the term, "mentoring." *Mentoring & Tutoring: Partnership in Learning*, *24*, 1–7. doi:10.1080/13611267.2016.1170556

Ito, M., Baumer, S., Bittanti, M., boyd, d., Cody, R., Herr-Stephenson, B., … Tripp, L. (2010). *Hanging out, messing around, and geeking out: Kids living and learning with new media*. Cambridge, MA: MIT Press.

Ito, M., Gutiérrez, K., Livingstone, S., Penuel, B., Rhodes, J., Salen, K., … Watkins, S. C. (2013). *Connected learning: An agenda for research and design*. Retrieved from Digital Media and Learning Research Hub website: https://dmlhub.net/publications/connected-learning-agenda-for-research-and-design/

Jacobi, M. (1991). Mentoring and undergraduate academic success: A literature review. *Review of Educational Research*, *61*, 505–532. doi:10.3102/00346543061004505

Jamison, A. E. (2013). *Fic: Why fanfiction is taking over the world*. Dallas, TX: Smart Pop.

Jarvis, S., & Daller, M. (2013). *Vocabulary Knowledge: Human ratings and automated measures*. Amsterdam, Netherlands: John Benjamins.

Jenkins, H. (1992). *Textual Poachers: Television fans and participatory culture.* New York, NY: Routledge.

Jenkins, H. (2006). *Convergence culture: Where old and new media collide.* New York, NY: New York University Press.

Jenkins, H. (2009). *Confronting the challenges of participatory culture: Media education for the 21st century.* Cambridge, MA: MIT Press.

Jenkins, H. (2012). "Cultural acupuncture": Fan activism and the *Harry Potter* Alliance. *Transformative Works and Cultures, 10.* doi:10.3983/twc.2012.0305

Johnson, S. F. (2014). Fan fiction metadata creation and utilization within fan fiction archives: Three primary models. *Transformative Works and Cultures, 17.* doi:10.3983/twc.2014.0578

Johnson, W., Fairbanks, H., Mann, M. B., & Chotlos, J. W. (1944). Studies in language behavior [Monograph]. *Psychological Monographs: General and Applied, 56*(2). doi:10.1037/h0093508

Johnston, J. E. (2015). *Doctor Who*–themed weddings and the performance of fandom. *Transformative Works and Cultures, 18.* doi:10.3983/twc.2015.0637

Jwa, S. (2012). Modeling L2 writer voice: Discoursal positioning in fanfiction writing. *Computers and Composition: An International Journal for Teachers of Writing, 29,* 323–340. doi:10.1016/j.compcom.2012.10.001

Katyal, S. (2006). Performance, property, and the slashing of gender in fan fiction. *American University Journal of Gender, Social Policy, and the Law, 14,* 461–518. Retrieved from https://digitalcommons.wcl.american.edu/jgspl/vol14/iss3/2/

Keller, T. E. (2005). The stages and development of mentoring relationships. In D. L. DuBois & M. J. Karcher (Eds.), *Handbook of youth mentoring* (pp. 82–99). Thousand Oaks, CA: Sage.

Kelley, B. (2016a). *To my betas, endless chocolate frogs! Exploring the intersections of emotion, the body, and literacy in online fanfiction* (Doctoral dissertation). Retrieved from https://ir.library.louisville.edu/etd/2474

Kelley, B. (2016b). Toward a goodwill ethics of online research methods. *Transformative Works and Cultures, 22.* doi:10.3983/twc.2016.0891

Khasnabis, D., Reischl, C. H., Stull, M., & Boerst, T. (2013). Distributed mentoring: Designing contexts for collective support of teacher learning. *English Journal, 102*(3), 71–77.

Kirschner, P., Strijbos, J.-W., Kreijns, K., & Beers, P. J. (2004). Designing electronic collaborative learning environments. *Educational Technology Research and Development, 52*(3), 47–66. doi:10.1007/BF02504675

Ko, A. J., & Davis, K. (2017). Computing mentorship in a software boomtown: Relationships to adolescent interest and beliefs. In J. Tenenberg, D. Chinn, J. Sheard, & L. Malmi (Chairs), *Proceedings of the 2017 ACM Conference on International Computing Education Research* (pp. 236–244). doi:10.1145/3105726.3106177

Ko, A. J., Hwa, L., Davis, K., & Yip, J. C. (2018). Informal mentoring of adolescents about computing: Relationships, roles, qualities, and impact. In T. Barnes, D. Garcia, E. K. Hawthorne, & M. A. Pérez-Quiñones (Chairs), *Proceedings of the 49th ACM Technical Symposium on Computer Science Education* (pp. 598–603). doi:10.1145/3159450.3159475

Kram, K. E. (1985). *Mentoring at work: Developmental relationships in organizational life.* Glenview, IL: Scott, Foresman.

Kreijns, K., & Kirschner, P. A. (2004) Designing sociable CSCL environments: Applying interaction design principles. In J. Strijbos, P. A. Kirschner, and R. L. Martens (Eds.), *What we know about CSCL and implementing it in higher education.* Boston, MA: Kluwer Academic.

Lammers, J. C. (2014). Fangirls as teachers: Examining pedagogic discourse in an online fan site. *Learning, Media and Technology, 38,* 368–386. doi:10.1080/17439884.2013.764895

Lammers, J. C. (2016). "The Hangout was serious business": Leveraging participation in an online space to design Sims fanfiction. *Research in the Teaching of English, 50,* 309–332. Retrieved from http://www.ncte.org/library/NCTEFiles/Resources/Journals/RTE/0503-feb2016/RTE0503Hangout.pdf

Lammers, J. C., & Marsh, V. L. (2015). Going public: An adolescent's networked writing on Fanfiction.net. *Journal of Adolescent & Adult Literacy, 59,* 277–285. doi:10.1002/jaal.416

Lankshear, C., & Knobel, M. (2007). Researching new literacies: Web 2.0 practices and insider perspectives. *E-Learning, 4,* 224–240. doi:10.2304/elea.2007.4.3.224

Larbalestier, J. (2002). *The battle of the sexes in science fiction.* Middletown, CT: Wesleyan University Press.

Latagne, S. M. (2011). The better angels of our fanfiction: The need for true and logical precedent. *Hastings Communications and Entertainment Law Journal, 33,* 159–481. Retrieved from https://repository.uchastings.edu/hastings_comm_ent_law_journal/vol33/iss2/1/

Lave, J., & Wenger, E. (1991). *Situated learning: Legitimate peripheral participation.* Cambridge, England: Cambridge University Press.

Lessig, L. (2004). *Free culture: How big media uses technology and the law to lock down culture and control creativity.* New York, NY: Penguin Press.

Lessig, L. (2008). *Remix: Making art and commerce thrive in the hybrid economy*. New York, NY: Penguin Press.

Levinson, D. J. (1979). *The seasons of a man's life*. New York, NY: Ballantine Books.

Mackey, M., & McClay, J. K. (2008). Pirates and poachers: Fan fiction and the conventions of reading and writing. *English in Education, 42*, 131–147. doi:10.1111/j.1754-8845.2008.00011.x

Malvern, D., Richards, B., Chipere, N., & Durán, P. (2004). *Lexical diversity and language development: Quantification and assessment*. Basingstoke, England: Palgrave Macmillan.

Mathew, K. L., & Adams, D. C. (2009). I love your book, but I love my version more: Fanfiction in the English language arts classroom. *The ALAN Review, 36*(3), 35–41. doi:10.21061/alan.v36i3.a.5

Mazgutova, D., & Kormos, J. (2015). Syntactic and lexical development in an intensive English for Academic Purposes programme. *Journal of Second Language Writing, 29*, 3–15. doi:10.1016/j.jslw.2015.06.004

McCardle, M. (2003). Fan fiction, fandom, and fanfare: What's all the fuss? *Boston University Journal of Science and Technology Law, 9*(2), 433–470. Retrieved from http://www.bu.edu/law/journals-archive/scitech/volume92/mccardle.pdf

McCarthy, P. M., & Jarvis, S. (2010). MTLD, vocd-D, and HD-D: A validation study of sophisticated approaches to lexical diversity assessment. *Behavior Research Methods, 42*, 381–392. doi:10.3758/BRM.42.2.381

McKee, G., Malvern, D., & Richards, B. (2000). Measuring vocabulary diversity using dedicated software. *Literary and Linguistic Computing, 15*, 323–338. doi:10.1093/llc/15.3.323

McNamara, D. S., Crossley, S. A., & McCarthy, P. M. (2010). Linguistic features of writing quality. *Written Communication, 27*, 57–86. doi:10.1177/0741088309351547

Merriam, S. B. (2009). *Qualitative research: A guide to design and implementation*. San Francisco, CA: Jossey-Bass.

Merrick, H. (2009). *The secret feminist cabal: A cultural history of science fiction feminisms*. Seattle, WA: Aqueduct Press.

Meyrowitz, J. (1985). *No sense of place: The impact of electronic media on social behavior*. New York, NY: Oxford University Press.

Miles, M. B., & Huberman, A. M. (1994). *Qualitative data analysis: An expanded sourcebook*. Thousand Oaks, CA: Sage.

Milli, S., & Bamman, D. (2016). Beyond canonical texts: A computational analysis of fanfiction. In J. Su, X. Carreras, & K. Duh (Chairs), *Proceedings of the 2016 Conference on Empirical Methods in Natural Language Processing* (pp. 2048–2053). Retrieved from https://www.aclweb.org/anthology/D/D16/D16-1218.pdf

Moore, M. J., Nakano, T., Enomoto, A., & Suda, T. (2012). Anonymity and roles associated with aggressive posts in an online forum. *Computers in Human Behavior, 28*, 861–867. doi:10.1016/j.chb.2011.12.005

Moretti, F. (2000). Conjectures on world literature. *New Left Review, 1*, 54–68. Retrieved from https://newleftreview.org/II/1/franco-moretti-conjectures-on-world-literature

Moretti, F. (2013). *Distant reading*. London, England: Verso.

Murray, M. (2001). *Beyond the myths and magic of mentoring: How to facilitate an effective mentoring process*. San Francisco, CA: Jossey-Bass.

Musiani, F. (2011). Editorial policies, "public domain," and acafandom. *Transformative Works and Cultures, 7*. doi:10.3983/twc.2011.0275

Neuman, S. B., & Celano, D. (2012). *Giving our children a fighting chance: Poverty, literacy, and the development of information capital*. New York, NY: Teachers College Press.

Nolan, M. E. (2006). Search for original expression: Fan fiction and the fair use defense. *Southern Illinois University Law Journal, 30*, 533–571.

Olinghouse, N. G., & Wilson, J. (2013). The relationship between vocabulary and writing quality in three genres. *Reading and Writing, 26*, 45–65. doi:10.1007/s11145-012-9392-5

Organisation for Economic Cooperation and Development. (2016). *PISA 2015 Results: Vol. 1. Excellence and equity in education*. doi:10.1787/9789264266490-en

Out of Eden Learn. (n.d.). About us. Retrieved January 29, 2019, from https://learn.outofedenwalk.com/about/

Parrish, J. (2007). *Inventing a universe: Reading and writing internet fan fiction* (Doctoral dissertation). Retrieved from http://d-scholarship.pitt.edu/8963/

Penley, C. (1997). *NASA/TREK: Popular science and sex in America*. New York, NY: Verso.

Pidgeon, N., & Henwood, K. (1996). Grounded theory: Practical implementation. In J. T. E. Richardson (Ed.), *Handbook of qualitative research and methods for psychology and the social sciences* (pp. 86–101). Oxford, England: BPS Blackwell.

Project Gutenberg. (2018). Retrieved May 25, 2018, from http://www.gutenberg.org/

Reich, J. E. (2015, July 23). Fanspeak: The brief origins of fanfiction. *Tech Times*. Retrieved from http://www.techtimes.com/articles/70108/20150723/fan-fiction-star-trek-harry-potter-history-of-fan-fiction-shakespeare-roman-mythology-greek-mythology-sherlock-holmes.htm

Rhodes, J. E., Grossman, J. B., & Roffman, J. (2002). The rhetoric and reality of youth mentoring. In J. E. Rhodes (Ed.), *New directions for youth development: Theory, practice, and research: A critical view of youth mentoring* (pp. 9–20). San Francisco, CA: Jossey-Bass.

Rhodes, J. E., & Lowe, S. R. (2009). Mentoring in adolescence. In R. M. Lerner & L. D. Steinberg (Eds.), *Handbook of Adolescent Psychology: Vol. 2. Contextual influences on adolescent development* (pp. 152–190). Hoboken, NJ: Wiley.

Ringland, K. E., Wolf, C. T., Boyd, L. E., Baldwin, M. S., & Hayes, G. R. (2016). Would you be mine: Appropriating *Minecraft* as an assistive technology for youth with autism. In J. H. Feng & M. Huenerfauth (Chairs), *Proceedings of the 18th International ACM SIGACCESS Conference on Computers and Accessibility* (pp. 33–41). doi:10.1145/2982142.2982172

Roberts, A. (2000). Mentoring revisited: A phenomenological reading of the literature. *Mentoring & Tutoring: Partnership in Learning, 8*, 145–170. doi:10.1080/713685524

Rogoff, B. (1998). Cognition as a collaborative process. In D. Kuhn, R. S. Siegler, & W. Damon (Eds.), *Handbook of Child Psychology: Vol. 2. Cognition, perception, and language* (5th ed., pp. 679–744). New York, NY: Wiley.

Romano, Aja. (2010, May 3). I'm done explaining why fanfic is okay [Blog post]. Retrieved from https://bookshop.livejournal.com/1044495.html

Roozen, K. (2009). "Fan Fic-ing" English studies: A case study exploring the interplay of vernacular literacies and disciplinary engagement. *Research in the Teaching of English, 44*, 136–169. Retrieved from https://www.jstor.org/stable/27784355

Roschelle, J., & Teasley, S. D. (1995). The construction of shared knowledge in collaborative problem solving. In C. O'Malley (Ed.), *Computer supported collaborative learning* (pp. 69–97). Berlin, Germany: Springer-Verlag.

Sandherr, J., Roberson, A., Martin, C. K., Acholonu, U., & Nacu, D. (2014). *Distributed mentorship: Increasing and diversifying youth access to learning networks.* Panel at the 6th Annual Digital Media and Learning Conference, Boston, MA.

Scales, P., & Leffert, N. (1999). *Developmental assets: A synthesis of the scientific research on adolescent development.* Minneapolis, MN: Search Institute.

Schwabach, A. (2009). The *Harry Potter* lexicon and the world of fandom: Fan fiction, outsider works, and copyright. *University of Pittsburgh Law Review, 70*, 387–434.

Schwabach, A. (2011). *Fan fiction and copyright: Outside works and intellectual property protection.* Burlington, VT: Ashgate.

Scodari, C. (2004). *Serial monogamy: Soap opera, lifespan, and the gendered politics of fantasy.* Cresskill, NJ: Hampton Press.

Selman, R. L. (1975). Level of social perspective taking and the development of empathy in children: Speculations from a social-cognitive viewpoint. *Journal of Moral Education, 5*, 35–43. doi:10.1080/0305724750050105

Sendlor, C. (2011, March 18). Fan fiction demographics in 2010: Age, sex, country [Blog post]. Retrieved from http://ffnresearch.blogspot.com/2011/03/fan-fiction-demographics-in-2010-age.html

Silbereisen, R., & Lerner, R. M. (2007). *Approaches to positive youth development.* Los Angeles, CA: Sage.

Sims, C. (2014). From differentiated use to differentiating practices: Negotiating legitimate participation and the production of privileged identities. *Information, Communication & Society, 17*, 670–682. doi:10.1080/1369118X.2013.808363

Smagorinsky, P. (2008). The method section as conceptual epicenter in constructing social science research reports. *Written Communication, 25*, 389–411. doi:10.1177/0741088308317815

Snyder, T. D., de Brey, C., & S. A. Dillow. (2018). *Digest of educational statistics 2016* (NCES 2017-094). Retrieved from https://nces.ed.gov/pubs2017/2017094.pdf

Speer, J. B. (1944). *Fancyclopedia.* Los Angeles, CA: Forrest J. Ackerman for the Los Angeles Science Fantasy Society.

Stahl, G., Koschmann, T., & Suthers, D. D. (2006). Computer-supported collaborative learning: An historical perspective. In R. K. Sawyer (Ed.), *Cambridge Handbook of the Learning Sciences* (pp. 409–426). Cambridge, England: Cambridge University Press.

Steiner, P. (1993, July 5). On the internet [Cartoon]. *The New Yorker.* Retrieved from https://condenaststore.com/featured/on-the-internet-peter-steiner.html

Steinkuehler, C., & Duncan, S. (2008). Scientific habits of mind in virtual worlds. *Journal of Science Education and Technology, 17*, 530–543. doi:10.1007/s10956-008-9120-8

Stendell, L. (2005). Fanfic and fan fact: How current copyright law ignores the reality of copyright owner and consumer interests in fan fiction. *SMU Law Review, 58*, 1551–1581. Retrieved from https://scholar.smu.edu/smulr/vol58/iss4/9/

Stroude, R. L. (2010). Complimentary creation: Protecting fan fiction as fair use. *Marquette Intellectual Property Law Review, 14*, 191–213. Retrieved from https://scholarship.law.marquette.edu/iplr/vol14/iss1/11/

Svensson, P. (2010). The landscape of digital humanities. *Digital Humanities Quarterly, 4*(1). Retrieved from http://digitalhumanities.org/dhq/vol/4/1/000080/000080.html

Theokas, C., & Lerner, R. M. (2006). Observed ecological assets in families, schools, and neighborhoods: Conceptualization, measurement, and relations with positive and negative developmental outcomes. *Applied Developmental Science, 10*, 61–74. doi:10.1207/s1532480xads1002_2

Tosenberger, C. (2008). Homosexuality at the online Hogwarts: *Harry Potter* slash fanfiction. *Children's Literature, 36*, 185–207. doi:10.1353/chl.0.0017

Treffers-Daller, J. (2013). Measuring lexical diversity among L2 learners of French: An exploration of the validity of D, MTLD and HD-D as measures of language ability. In S. Jarvis & M. Daller (Eds.), *Vocabulary knowledge: Human ratings and automated measures* (pp. 79–104). Amsterdam, Netherlands: John Benjamins Publishing.

Turkle, S. (2011). *Alone together: Why we expect more from technology and less from each other*. New York, NY: Basic Books.

Tushnet, R. (1997). Legal fictions: Copyright, fan fiction, and a new common law. *Loyola of Los Angeles Entertainment Law Journal, 17*, 651–686. Retrieved from https://digitalcommons.lmu.edu/elr/vol17/iss3/8/

Tushnet, R. (2009). Economies of desire: Fair use and marketplace assumptions. *William & Mary Law Review, 51*, 513–546. Retrieved from https://scholarship.law.wm.edu/wmlr/vol51/iss2/6/

Tushnet, R. (2017). Copyright law, fan practices, and the rights of the author. In J. Gray, C. Sandvoss, & C. L. Harrington (Eds.), *Fandom: Identities and communities in a mediated world* (pp. 60–71). New York, NY: New York University Press.

Twenge, J. (2017). *iGen: Why today's super-connected kids are growing up less rebellious, more tolerant, less happy—and completely unprepared for adulthood (and what that means for the rest of us)*. New York, NY: Atria Books.

US Department of Education, Institute of Education Sciences, National Center for Education Statistics. (2012). *The nation's report card: Writing 2011* (NCES 2012–470). Retrieved from https://nces.ed.gov/nationsreportcard/pdf/main2011/2012470.pdf

Veale, K. (2013). Capital, dialogue, and community engagement: *My Little Pony: Friendship Is Magic* understood as an alternate reality game. *Transformative Works and Cultures, 14*. doi:10.3983/twc.2013.0510

Walther, J. B. (1996). Computer-mediated communication: Impersonal, interpersonal, and hyperpersonal interaction. *Communication Research, 23*, 3–43. doi:10.1177/009365096023001001

Walther, J. B. (2011). Theories of computer-mediated communication and interpersonal relations. In M. L. Knapp & J. A. Daly (Eds.), *The Sage handbook of interpersonal communication* (pp. 443–479). Thousand Oaks, CA: Sage.

Weinstein, E. C., Clark, Z., DiBartolomeo, D. J., & Davis, K. (2014). A decline in creativity? It depends on the domain. *Creativity Research Journal, 26*, 174–184. doi:10.1080/10400419.2014.901082

West, J. (2014, November 2). None of this is new: An oral history of fanfiction. *The Mary Sue.* Retrieved from https://www.themarysue.com/none-of-this-is-new-an-oral-history-of-fanfiction/

White, R. H. (2014). *Lexical richness in adolescent writing, insights from the classroom: An L1 vocabulary development study* (Master's thesis, Victoria University of Wellington, Wellington, New Zealand). Retrieved from http://researcharchive.vuw.ac.nz/handle/10063/3394

Whiteman, N. (2012). *Undoing ethics: Rethinking practice in online research.* New York, NY: Springer.

Witten, I. H., Frank, E., & Hall, M. A. (2011). *Data mining: Practical machine learning tools and techniques* (3rd ed.). Amsterdam, Netherlands: Morgan Kaufmann.

Yin, K., Aragon, C., Evans, S., & Davis, K. (2017). Where no one has gone before: A meta-dataset of the world's largest fanfiction repository. In G. Mark, S. Fussell, C. Lampe, m. c. schraefel, J. P. Hourcade, C. Appert, & D. Wigdor (Chairs), *Proceedings of the 2017 CHI Conference on Human Factors in Computing Systems* (pp. 6106–6110). doi:10.1145/3025453.3025720

Yu, G. (2010). Lexical diversity in writing and speaking task performances. *Applied Linguistics, 31*, 236–259. doi:10.1093/applin/amp024

Zook, M., Barocas, S., boyd, d., Crawford, K., Keller, E., S. P. Gangadharan, ... Pasquale, F. (2017). Ten simple rules for responsible big data research [Editorial]. *PLoS Computational Biology, 13*(3), e1005399. doi:10.1371/journal.pcbi.1005399

Index

Page numbers followed by *f* or *t* refer to figures or tables, respectively.